A FEW SHORT STORIES

Short Stories to Inspire Writing Topics

T Lee Sizemore

This is a work of non-fiction.
Text and Illustrations copyrighted
by T Lee Sizemore, DVM, RN ©2016

Library of Congress Control Number: 2016919898

All rights reserved. No part of this book may be reproduced, transmitted, or stored in an information retrieval
system in any form or by any means, graphic, electronic, or mechanical without prior written
permission from the author.

First Edition 2016

Printed in the United States of America
A 2 Z Press LLC
PO Box 582
Deleon Springs, FL 32130
bestlittleonlinebookstore.com
bestlittleonlinebookstore@gmailcom
386-681-7402

ISBN: 978-0-9976407-8-6

Dedication

This book is dedicated in memory
of my beloved grandfather,
Alexander Balcziunas.

INTRODUCTION

Writers write. It's a fact I learned many years ago. However, sometimes, writers have 'writer's block' where it is difficult to know what to write about.

This short book is filled with personal stories for those who want something short to read at bedtime or share with others. It is also intended for those who would like to write themselves. Sections follow each story for space for a budding writer to put their thoughts and experiences on paper. Sometimes stories we decide to write are similar to those we read and sometimes they are very different. Something in the story can spark a similar or completely different memory. There are no rules in this book. Write what you want to. Read only if you want to.

The author just hopes you will enjoy the stories she wrote as she remembered the most amazing times in her life.

My First Rescue

Each Saturday, when I was fourteen years old, I took a bus to a church on the near West side of Cleveland. I worked with the local children and shut ins. One Saturday after finishing with the children, I visited a local animal shelter.

Row after row of begging dogs and cats in cages called to me to bust them out and take them home. The site of these pets broke my heart.

After walking down all the rows of animals, on my way out, a family was on their way in with a black cat in their arms. I gasped and blurted – as I usually did when caught by surprise - 'Are you taking that cat in there?'

"Yes," they relied, and continued, "why, do you want her?"

I said, "Yes."

I boarded the public bus with that cat in my arms, which then sat in my lap the 10 mile ride home, and the bus driver never said a word.

Without any real plan, I arrived home and decided to hide her in my room. As everyone with a cat knows, she did not stay hidden long. Thankfully, my mother is an avid animal lover also and she took care of her since I did not have a job and no way to make money to feed her.

Several years later, my mom commented to me, 'She seems to be so grateful.' I then shared that cat's story with my mom. I think every animal rescued is grateful.

Write your story here

4th of July Fireworks

As a veterinarian, many clients share with me how their pets are frightened by fireworks. One couple I am friends with shared their story with me so I could share with you. Over the years they have had many dogs and have always known of the common issue of fear many dogs experience with the loud noise of fireworks.

Since their home sits in the direct path of the booming sounds and the flashing lights and the fizzles of fireworks, they wanted to make certain their new pet, Sadie would not be afraid. The entire light show can be seen from their living room.

So, when Sadie, was a puppy, to prepare her. They sat with her during the entire fireworks display, pet her gently, and said, "Gooooood Sadie," in soft soothing voices. As they gave her treats and made this a 'happy' and safe time, she became less and less fearful of the fireworks.

After many years, Sadie was able to sit with my friends in their driveway as they all enjoyed the fun of the fireworks together. Their son commented on how calm she was during the display!

While this worked for Sadie, their neighbors chose to take their pet away during the fireworks. Since the neighbor was as close to the display as my friends, he chose to avoid the event altogether because of the distress he noted in his dog. We are not sure where he takes his dog, but we know he is a thoughtful owner.

In addition, clients have told me thunder shirts have helped their pets react less to fireworks as well as storm thunder and lightning. Others have chosen medications. However you help, we hope it helps. Our pets need to know they are safe.

I have a little dog Fluffy. She seems content to hide under the bed.

A friend of mine told me she left her home one 4th of July with her dog inside. When she returned, she discovered he was so frightened by the noise of the fireworks he damaged a screen in a window, escaped, and was nowhere to be found. She was frantic wondering if he was ok.

She received a phone call from a local CVS- turned out, he ran down her street, across a busy street in her neighborhood, and triggered the door to enter. He had tags with his name and phone number on, so they called her to inform her he was safe and there.

When she arrived, he ran to her immediately with his tail wagging. The store personnel had been feeding him treats to keep him calm while they waited for her to pick him up. She was thankful for their kindness and for him being safe as well. She never left home on fireworks night again.

Write your story here

The Amazing Things They Do

When the recession hit several years ago, one Ohio friend and her husband sought employment in West Virginia. They decided to make it an adventure and traveled there in an RV with their two dogs.

They had an aged dog named Shelby. I knew Shelby well because I was her veterinarian for many years. Now she was at the point in her long life that she slept most of the time and had slight difficulty getting up sometimes.

They also had a spry young little pup named Penny. Penny had enough energy for 5 dogs to tell the truth.

While in West Virginia over the summer months, It was quite hot one day. Shelby was resting on a blanket in the RV when my friend saw Penny take hold of the water bowl with her paw and drag it across the floor to her friend, Shelby. Amazing and thoughtful for sure.

When they returned to their Ohio home, I visited and learned that each day my friend came home from wherever she had been she would give both dogs treats. One day upon her arrival home, Penny met her at the door for her treat. After taking the treat, the pup ran into the other room but returned quickly looking for another treat.

My friend told Penny, 'No, I gave you a treat, this one is for Shelby.'

When she went into the room where Shelby was, she discovered that Penny had delivered the first treat she was given to Shelby. Penny did receive another treat and told what a very good girl she was.

It always amazes me how often I am surprised by the wonderful things dogs do.
They always seem to be thinking.

Write your story here_____

Water Thirsty Animals

Every spring I plant a little vegetable garden. Every year I get a little better at it. I learned how to safely keep the deer away and still maintain an organic garden. But we are always at the mercy of the weather. You see, Ohio weather can be brutal: snow in May, a soggy June, and now a dry, hot July. So I wait for the fruits of my labor, the cucumbers, the zucchini, the peppers and the most coveted prize, the tomatoes.   Friends, the bright green tomatoes look great and with the hot weather they will be ripening them soon. I have a tradition to take the first red tomato and make the world's best BLT. Unfortunately that would be a few days away. But I had a small tomato plant with cherry tomatoes that were ready and I had a salad planned for dinner.

When I went to pick those ripened cherry tomatoes, I started seeing half eaten tomatoes all over the ground. Who could do such a thing? The next day, I asked someone at work why, all of a sudden, would the chipmunks start eating my tomatoes? They smiled and answered-how obvious –they are thirsty.

This made me think about all the heat that grips this country in July. We have to think of the animals. Keep your water bowls filled. Add some ice cubes if they are out in the heat. Even if you don't have pets outside, a small bowl of water just might keep the chipmunks and squirrels from raiding your precious and delightful garden! Stay cool everyone!!!

Write your story here_____

Gale's Story – What Do Our Pets Do When We Are Away?

One weekend I went to see the movie "The Secret Life of Pets." It was positively delightful. But it made me think about what my pets do all day. Oh it is easy to think all they do is sleep. But every time I pull in, there is my cat Newman at the door waiting for me.

Back in the day, when my daughter was small, she would receive a Christmas gift from the dog or cat currently in our family. Usually her gifts were pajamas or slippers, but always something. One year, she asked me how the dog got out to go shopping.

"I don't know. I'm at work all day," I answered. But I like the idea of the pets heading down to the local Target, looking for the right gift, hoping it is on sale, using my Target card to get the 5% discount. Maybe they have a pet discount day like they do for seniors. Do they get distracted walking by the pet aisles, checking out the new treats and toys? Don't dawdle too long - you have to be back home before your human gets home.

What do you think happens at your house while you are gone?

Write your story here _____

Worst Day Ever

One day as a large animal veterinarian, (code for horse doctor), I responded to a call for a trailer accident with 2 horses trapped. The car pulling the trailer did not negotiate a hill. This resulted in the trailer tipping over on its side. The fire department also responded. None of the young women in the car were injured, and the firemen and I successfully removed one of the horses with minimal injury from the trailer. We tried everything to free the second horse, but were unable to do so.

As I watched the horse struggling and injuring itself on the metal parts in the trailer, I decided the only way we could get that horse out of that trailer was for me to use field anesthesia.

First I gave a sedative, then followed with a short acting anesthetic. When used in the field, I was able to lay the horse on the ground, do my procedure, wait a short time, and then the horse wake up and stand on their own. Easy-peasy most of the time.

I shared my plan with the firemen. They were on board. After administering the medication the horse stopped struggling, relaxed, and was sedated as planned. Since firemen arrive with water in their trucks, we sprayed water on the horse, the ramp of the trailer, and as much under the horse as we could. Then we – me and 6 strong men – pulled the horse free of the trailer.

It was a relief to have the horse free. One problem was solved, but another was just beginning. Being forced to recover this horse on the road presented significant challenges. There were ditches on both sides of this country road and, as I began to recover him, he tried to get up too soon. The short acting anesthesia is short acting, but it does need some time to clear the body and allow the horse to stand without being wobbly.

As the horse began to wake up sooner than able, he stumbled and rolled off the road and into the ditch. He continued to try to get up too soon and continued to roll down the ditch into a ravine and into the water at the bottom of the ravine. Because horses are so large, there was no way I could stop this. With the riders of the horse standing close watching me and all that was happening, I kept thinking 'this just keeps getting better.'

Unable to speak, I stood praying he would not break a leg or his neck. I knew he was an athlete, but this just kept getting worse. His rider and I jumped down into the ravine We stood on each side of him with ropes. I had her place a towel across his face in the hope that he would just stop trying to walk until more of the medication wore off.

Finally he was steadier on this hooves. In his athletic jumping fashion, he bunny hopped up the incline out of the ravine out of the ditch to the road level. He was still a little wobbly, but walking well enough to not endanger himself or any of us handling him. We found a nearby farm that allowed us to use a stall to repair the injuries he sustained in the accident. I spent two hours repairing cuts and medicating him. He may not have been able to do his show jumping that day, but soon afterward he was back in saddle again- so to say.

I am thankful that all worked out in the end even though I was never more terrified in my life for all the events that happened this day.

Write your story here____

Training My Dogs

There are some very talented people I am certain could train a dog to do anything. I, on the other hand, fear I could not train a Spaniel to stay. I realized my shortcoming a long time ago.

When I was a little girl, our family pet was a Doberman/Shepherd cross. She was very smart and I trained her to stay, jump a small stick held by buckets, fetch, and other tricks. Looking back, I don't think her learning had anything to do with my training talents, I think she just really had a knack for knowing what to do. Some dogs are like that - they seem to train themselves.

I have friends who train their dogs for search and rescue. Some train them for showing or herding animals. We all know some dogs are service dogs- these are talents that continually amaze me.

Over the past many years, I have owned many dogs. When clients ask me about training issues with their pets, I share with them that I am truly not a trainer, my knowledge is in medicine. We share our stories and they laugh when I tell them my dogs only know 'cookie' and 'bye-bye.' I add that sometimes they even come to me when I call them. My present dog is a Blue Heeler Rudy. He is a prime example of this. He hears me call him, he looks my way, and then promptly goes the other way! Little stinker.

One evening several years ago, my dogs were all sleeping on various blankets scattered on my living room floor. When my phone call with a friend ended, I said 'bye bye'. Suddenly, all eleven of my dogs jumped up and ran to me with smiling faces and wagging tails as if to say, "Yes, we want to go bye-bye." THAT they respond to. We did go 'bye- bye' and then had 'cookies.' My dogs may have only a little training, but they are great dogs.

Share the tricks you've taught your dogs.

Write your story here_____

Harriet

It was a normal day at the clinic that morning – filled with surgeries and office appointments. During all the hustle and bustle, in came the Animal Control lady with a small kitten.

"We found this kitten in a storm drain," she said. "Do you think anyone would want her?" The kitten just fit in her hand.

I stopped working and said, "Let me take a look at her."

As I examined her, I noticed the usual stray kitten problems- goopy eyes, discharge from the nose, and frightened. This little girl also had fly larvae in her back end area. This is a serious problem and sometimes too advanced to save a pet.

"I'll take her," I said. I named her Harriet.

I started her on antibiotics and began treating her fly larvae by flushing the area with hydrogen peroxide several times a day. Each time I did, more larvae were killed. When I flushed the areas, Harriet allowed me to flush, but she complained with short little 'mews' – not a full meow sound. I like to think she knew I was helping and I loved her and that's why she let me treat her.

After several days of treatments, all the fly larvae were gone. Next I treated intestinal parasites causing diarrhea. After treating all that and her eyes and nose, eventually she was healthy.

When Harriet was young, we lived alone on my farm. Because of this, she was not properly socialized. She and I played, but whenever we had company she hid until they left.

A few years ago, family needs took me to Florida. I asked my brother to care for Harriet thinking I would only be gone for 5 months. When I left her, she was inside my brother's home, but a few weeks later, she darted out an open door and refused to come to him or back into the house. I was devastated. She spent the entire harsh winter outside. My brother assured me he put food out for her and it was eaten, but we did not know if other animals ate it or she did. I was afraid she would be harmed or lost in the mountains around his home.

After ten very long months of separation, my brother brought her to me. We both agreed it was a miracle he was able to catch her, put her in a carrier, and bring her to me.

When she arrived, I took her into my bedroom, and began talking to her. She perked up and talked to me in kitten talk- little 'mews' to tell me how things were. I took her out of the carrier and as I held her, she curled up in my arms and many months of separation came to an end. My heart broke again and again as I imagined her outside wondering if I was coming back or what happened to me. Wondering if we were ever going to be together again and if she was going home. Harriet has convinced me that our pets know us and miss us very much when separated from us.

Every day since she and I have been reunited- 2years now, when I come home from anywhere, she greets me and snuggles close to my neck on my chest. She does not seem concerned whether I have work to do or not. She does not care if I need to make phone calls, clean the room, or exercise. She just wants to be close. In her mind she owns me and never wants to be separated again.

When I sleep on my side, she sleeps on my shoulder. Occasionally, I squint when she does this and I see her watching to see if my eyes are open. If I open my eyes, she kisses my face or touches me with her paw. She sits on my shoulder until I wake in the morning.

Since Harriet was neglected as a kitten before I rescued her, her teeth were decayed. When I did dental care, I removed all her teeth - all but the front teeth. What I find funny is that she has recovered well from the extractions, however, she loves to play and when she does, she bites me playfully - with her only remaining front teeth.

I made a promise to Harriet that I would never leave her again.

Write your story here

Race Day at the Fair

I raced harness horses for many years. It was a fantastic time in my life. There has been little to compare to the thrill of one of my horses crossing the finish line first.

One of my favorite places to race was the county fair. Because of this, I looked forward to fair season every year. Not only was it fun to race at the fairs, I felt closer to the race since the tracks are close to the barns we stabled at. Also, the entire fair was enthralling.

Once my horse and her equipment were unloaded, she was settled in her stall, and I retrieved her warm up pad with her number on it, I made my way to the fair.

The sounds of clanging and the rides going round and round were all around me. As I walked down rows of game booths and food stands, the smell of the 'fair food' invited me to partake. What would I have today? Would it be a gyro? Or a funnel cake? French fries covered in vinegar? - to name a few of my favorite great greasy fair foods.

As I visited each building, I saw all the ribbons awarded before the fair opened. The blue and red and other ribbons were displayed on the winning pictures, quilts, pies, cookies, cakes, and artwork the locals brought to the fair. I loved seeing what and who won first prize. Once I entered my own cross stitch piece. I wish I could say I won a blue ribbon, but....It was just fun to participate – so they say.

I always made sure I stopped by the 4-H building to see the creative vegetable art the children entered. They brought gourds dressed as farmers and carrots with faces painted on them. Watermelons were decorated - some with faces carved out like Halloween pumpkins were some of my favorites. I always thought, 'These kids have talent.'

The fair that was the blue ribbon winner for me was in Lancaster, Ohio. This fair had all the usual buildings and displays, but this fair was my fair to remember. As I strolled through the poultry building, the 4-H er's were preparing their chickens and roosters for show. Some girls had just given baths to the whitest hens I had ever seen. Then, using blow dryers, proceeded to dry them. I stood watching as these young girls waved their blow dryers over the chickens as the chickens submissively and agreeably let them. Their little eyes were half closed as the warm air blew at and over them. Their feathers blew under the flow of air coming at them as they were primped for show. They seemed to enjoy the whole process. While I was quite amazed, these 4-H er's seem to shrug that this was 'just another day at the chicken and rooster show.'

On the other side of the poultry barn, a young man had his rooster on a stump. He worked diligently cleaning the grooves in the rooster's feet with a toothbrush- he had to be perfect for show of course. What I found amazing was the rooster was not being held. He was just standing still and letting his young owner clean his grooves.

After enjoying each fair, I focused on my race horse. It was her turn to have my undivided attention. I brushed her, put her equipment on, warmed up, and then sent her to the start line. We were off! The race ran and sometimes we were even first across the finish line. Sometimes it was just great taking part in the sport- so they say.

Write your story here_____

Gone Fishin

I have only fished a few times- and that was when I was a young girl. Recently, my brother-in-law asked me to fish with him. He was injured in a motorcycle accident many years ago, so he has taught me to put the leaders on, the hooks on, the yucky bait on, the sinkers on, and tie the knots, cast, and open and throw the bail. He has educated me on test line- and needing large enough fishing line to keep the line from breaking if we ever caught something. I probably don't know enough to do all these things, but how does one say no to a paralyzed man? When I went to the store to purchase items, it was helpful when the young men were fisherman themselves. Lost is a word for me. Clueless is another word.

I often wondered how he could enjoy fishing. It seemed he was not able to do all the things necessary to fish. Nevertheless, we rigged a holder on his wheelchair to hold the rod after I cast the line into the ocean on the Daytona Beach pier we are on. He is so happy to sit on the pier for hours waiting patiently for a nibble.

I realize it's not only the fishing that he likes on the pier, but it is the social interaction that happens on the pier when he fishes. He loves to be around others enjoying themselves and fishing is something he enjoys too. The sound of the water coming in is pleasant and the pelicans fly by continuously - they spend their mornings as master fishermen themselves. My brother-in-law has some limited ability to reel in a fish in the event we catch something. He and a friend told me they actually did catch a fish one day, however, I think I require proof of this. Each time someone on the pier catches a fish, everyone gets excited and comes to see.

The true fisher story of this tiny little striped fish on the line I am holding is that we fish for hours without catching anything. When someone fishing on the pier catches a fish, we ask if we can hold it and take a picture so we look like we caught the little thing. He holds the pole, I hold the line, and we both pose for the picture.
It was a great day at the beach.

Write your story here_____

Surprised by Lady's Love

When I was a young girl, I dreamed of owning a horse. I read all the Walter Farley horse stories and cherished every page, however, I was the second child of six and my family did not have money for the luxury of a horse. I dreamed anyway. Each Christmas I told my parents I was certain this would be the Christmas I would find a saddle and bridle under the tree and directions to the barn where I could find my new horse. Each Christmas there were toys and clothes and other gifts, but no bridle, no saddle, and no horse.

I rode every time an opportunity came along. Then, the summer before my last year in nursing school, while just sitting around in my room, I said to myself, 'I am going to buy a horse today.' I did. I bought a quarter-type mare named Lady.

What I did not know was that Lady was 'spoiled.' This means she was not well mannered and unpredictable. She would quickly jump sideways as if afraid of objects and could turn on a dime. I did not have the skills needed to ride when she twisted her body this way or spun around on her back heels. I was convinced she did this to throw me off her back. I was afraid of her and would drive home after trying to ride her crying, 'I bought a horse I cannot ride.'

Once, when attempting to ride Lady around the grounds she was stabled at, she began to rear and move quickly from objects we were passing and scared me so badly I dismounted and tied her to the fence with her bridle on- a real 'no -no' in riding. I went back to the barn to ask someone who was not afraid of her to get her. As I shared my fears with a friend at the barn, he assured me I would be riding her everywhere in six months. I did not believe him, but he was right. I did learn to control her and ride her erratic movements, but she was not always fun and I wanted a horse I could enjoy.

I found a thoroughbred who was easy to ride and loved him immediately. He was kind and rode quietly and was a delight in every way. I was amazed when Lady pinned her ears and showed her teeth as I rode him past her stall. She only did this when the thoroughbred and I rode by. She never gave me the impression she knew who I was, that she knew I loved her, or that she loved me.

One sunny afternoon, a friend and I decided to ride the horses to a nearby park several roads away from the barn. He rode Lady and I rode the thoroughbred. I was trotting ahead of them - across a large field as a matter of fact- when I realized she dumped him and was running full speed - rider less with stirrups flapping in the wind- in the direction of the barn. I was frantic because all I could image was her being hit by a car or falling in the street with slippery metal shoes as she ran furiously down busy streets and across main roads to get back to her barn.

I started screaming, "LADY" "LADY, COME GIRL." To my surprise, she stopped, looked my way, and began running full speed in my direction. I continued to call her name and she came right to me and the thoroughbred. Relief is a small word to describe how I felt. Love is another word that surprised me that day. She really did know I was her owner and the one who cared for her and loved her. I saw her differently after that day. She became my Lady.

Write your story here____

Gale's Little Schnapps

Every Labor Day weekend the Cuyahoga County Fairgrounds has Oktoberfest.

One of the highlights is the wiener dog races. I love watching those little legs run as fast as they can.

Our family has always owned dachshunds. In 1968, we got our first doxie - Schnapps. He came as a puppy from Florida, actually riding on a plane before any of us. He loved to swim and would bark non-stop and bite at the splashes when we were in the pool. We would put him on an inner tube and he would float around the pool. He was very protective of all of us and his food and rawhide. Some might say he was a little 'nippy.' He was a natural at sitting up and begging. My sister taught him to say "por favor". She was the only one learning Spanish, so we had to take her word for it.

At Christmas time, my mom would bake cookies during the day and hide them so we wouldn't eat them before Christmas. One year, Schnapps found a box of chocolate chip cookies hidden in her closet, and helped himself. His little belly was so full and we worried he would be sick - and this was before we knew chocolate was bad for dogs. He lived fortunately, although my mother sure wanted to kill him that night.

I used to have a gerbil named Spanky which I kept in a small aquarium. Sometimes, if something had spilled in the oven, the smoke alarm would go off at the top of our stairs. Schnapps would dart up the stairs, go right to the gerbil aquarium, and start barking and poking his nose right on the glass until the alarm stopped. He thought the gerbil was making that noise. I never said he was smart.

Schnapps never raced at Oktoberfest. I bet he would have been a contender while in his prime. I think he was about 12 when he died. We buried him in the backyard - a little area we called the pet cemetery. I wondered how he felt being buried near Spanky. He probably said something smart like, "Hey rat, I don't want any more noise from you." Schnapps - always had a little attitude.

Thank you Gale for sharing about Schnapps. We welcome our friends to share their stories of a favorite pet with us.

Write your story here____

Madeline

Nothing is more fun than a new pup. Madeline was a Golden Retriever that came to me. I called that little yellow ball of fluff my 'Princess Madeline.' She quickly became part of the family and seemed to just know what to do. She grew to be beautiful as well as smart. I wanted others to have a Madeline of their own. So I planned to make her a mommy.

Madeline had three litters for me, totaling 30 pups. Her first litter came one Christmas Eve. I was working as a nurse that evening when I received a call she was beginning to deliver. I arrived home just before midnight. She was nervous, so she and I spent the entire night together on the kitchen floor delivering those 10 beautiful babies. She seemed so confused each time one would come along. I assured her it was all 'ok' as I helped her with each pup. I slept on the kitchen floor next to her and she woke me each time the next new addition arrived. She quickly caught on to motherhood.

Her next litter was easier. She was experienced then. These 10 were darling pups as well and made many families happy.

Her third litter came after we moved to our 30 acre farm in North Central Ohio. The apartment we lived in was small, so I put her and the pups in the barn in a pen designed for fair ducks, but large enough to house everyone. When it came time for weaning, I began finding the pups homes. I was always pleasantly amazed how the perfect people came along to take each one of the pups. One by one, new owners took the puppies until the last pup was sold. Afterward, I looked everywhere, but could not find Madeline. When I searched the barn, I found her sitting in the pen all by herself looking at me as if to ask, 'Where are the babies?'" It broke my heart to tell her they were all gone.

Madeline was not only the mother of thirty pups, she was my best dog and the caretaker of our farm. She kept all unwanteds from the barn- the skunk, raccoons, 'possums, fox, coyotes, and most of all, the groundhogs. She knew the difference between my domestic rabbits and the wild rabbits in the yard. She never harmed my bunnies that ran freely around the barn- she actually protected them. There were times she would come into the barn and I could see little wild bunny legs hanging from her mouth.

I scolded her and told her she was not supposed to hurt them. She would wag her tail and smile as if to say, 'But they are soooooo good mama.' I could not be mad at her. She also brought home deer parts hunters left in the woods behind our farm. These little quirks disturbed me greatly and I was unprepared for them because I was a city girl. Suddenly, we were farmers - imposters actually- and here we were on a farm in the country. She was doing things farm dogs do that she would never do in the city. She was having a blast while I was saying 'ick.'

She not only watched over the barn, she made friends with the neighbors. As always, there is a time to say hello and a time to say good-bye. As Madeline advanced in age, she developed tumors that could not be treated. One day she and I were alone in the barn. I cried and hugged her. I thanked her for being my dog, for always greeting me when I came home, for making all the other animals safe and protecting the horses in the barn and all of us. I told her she was always dependable and meant more to me than I could even tell her. I told her how she made my life so great and happy and what a good girl she was. Then, I said good-bye.

It's always part of the deal. The more we love, the more it hurts when the time comes to say good-bye. I realized the only other option was to never love, but I did not choose that option. I have the memories of a lovely creature that came into my life and made it better. These memories make me happy.

Write your story here_____

Newbies

I have heard 'Even a fool who remains silent is thought to be wise.' Well, this may be so if no one ever finds out the truth. Wise and smart would not be the case for Amy and me as we survived our senior year in veterinary school touring farms in Columbus, Ohio.

I went to veterinary school to become a 'large animal' veterinarian. This actually translated into a 'horse' vet because I knew nothing about dairy, beef, pigs, sheep and goats, chickens and all the large animal industries.

Amy and I accompanied the instructors doing farm calls. During a visit to a local dairy we acted like experts as we nodded as if we understood everything being said and everything going on. The truth was we didn't really know that much.

We learned quickly though. The dairy cows spent most of their day out on pasture. When it was milking time, they lined up and walked into the 'milk parlor.' The milk parlor was a concrete floor with a large recessed area in the middle - something like a dugout in baseball. This is where the farmers stood - literally at 'udder level'- and, as the cows came in, lined up, and began eating at large troughs at their particular stations in the parlor, they attached the milking apparatuses to each cow's udders.

After giving many gallons of milk that was collected into a 'bulk tank,' the cows were released back to the pasture. The next cows repeated the process. The cows knew the routine. The milk collected in the 'bulk tank' was picked up and transported to dairies for processing- so we all 'got milk' and butter and yogurt and cheese and other dairy products.

During the milking this particular day, Amy and I watched the process quietly in the 'dugout.' The farmer and our instructor were talking. Suddenly, everyone quickly moved out and away from the cows – everyone except Amy and me. We stood motionless wondering where they were all going.

Suddenly, we were being splattered with soft, pudding consistency, cow patty manure. Manure was splashing in our faces and all over our coveralls. Everyone else noticed the cow lifting her tail – giving notice of the impending stool droppings. Apparently no one thought they needed to let us in on this little secret. We looked like the newbies we were. Everyone laughed as we tried our best to clean up.

Another day, we rode with the zoo veterinarian and visited the reptile building. Amy and I didn't care much for reptiles, so we stood behind the zoo vet observing the handlers bringing legless lizards and assorted other reptiles to the veterinarian for examination and care. Suddenly, we heard an alligator hiss. It sounded like it was right behind us! Amy jumped. I jumped. Everyone started laughing. "A little nervous are ya?" they asked. The truth was we were petrified and we believed for that moment that gator was on our side of the wall and it was actually behind the wall. Amy and I just shrugged and called it a day. Newbies we were. We managed to complete all our farm and zoo calls.

Write your story here_____

It is important that kitties and cats eat!

I have always known the two most frequent reasons for kitten loss are (1) a kitten becoming cold - because they are too young and small to maintain their body temperature and (2) low blood sugar. This is a concern because kittens do not have large amounts of 'fat' in their bodies to break down to sugar that is used as an energy source. Low body temperatures and low blood sugars are a serious concern to young kittens (and puppies as well).

While working at one veterinary clinic, I noticed a small black and white kitten in one of the cages. This little guy was underweight, had a dirty little face, and a runny little nose. Every day I visited his cage several times. Each time he would get up from reclining in his litter box, shake the litter from his body and leg, and come to the front of the cage to greet me. He purred and rubbed against the cage begging for attention. He did not realize how pathetic he appeared. One day I decided to take him home. I named him Mozart after my favorite composer.

Soon after Mozart came to live with me and my gang, I arrived home to find him down and out. He was cold and not responding well. I neglected to realize that while my apartment was warm enough for me and the other animals, it was not for Mo. He was young and underweight and he became cold. This happens sometimes with air conditioned homes as well. I quickly wrapped him in a blanket - papoose style- and grabbed a bottle of maple syrup- the only sugar substance I had in my apartment. I took him to my car because it was warm there with the sun coming through the windows. I placed small amounts of the syrup on his gums and slowly he began to respond. (Additional sugar sources found in our homes are honey, karo syrup, molasses, KMR-kitten milk replacer- and others). I never left him home alone again until he was old enough to eat well and had gained weight.

Mozart recovered well, but continued to have nasal discharge. I treated him with antibiotics and decongestants, however, there was no positive change in the discharge. The reason for the discharge is that he was infected with a respiratory virus prior to being vaccinated. I realize controversy exists regarding vaccinating cats, however, vaccines have proven to help minimize any damage to the sinuses if vaccinated before a cat or kitten is exposed to the virus. I still love Mozart, but he will always have nasal discharge. I encourage my cat and kitten clients to vaccinate their youngsters to avoid the lifelong nasal discharge.

In addition to kittens needing to eat to avoid low blood sugar, adult cats need to eat to avoid fatty livers. When cats mature, they usually have extra body fat. If a cat stops eating- for any reason- the fat in their bodies begins to break down because fat breaks down to sugar to be used for energy. This fat deposits in the liver. The condition of fat in the liver- hepatic lipidosis- is a serious condition in cats. If not treated and reversed, most cats affected are lost. I always make certain owners know their cats should eat regularly and if they stop eating, they need to see their veterinarian immediately for care.

It is important that kitties and cats eat!

Write your story here_____

Trick-or-treat

It was Halloween. I was in a hurry trying to finish all my veterinary house calls so I could get home in time to take my step daughter for trick or treating. We had such fun finding a costume for her and getting ready to go house to house in the neighborhood. This year she would be a princess- her favorite. She and I decorated the trees in the yard with ghosts made of Styrofoam balls and ripped up sheets. Pumpkins lined the drive. Each year we had a pumpkin carving party where we would invite all the neighborhood children to come for snacks and carving pumpkins. I was always amazed how the children would bring their little tools and get to carving. It was impossible to pick just one best carving when all the children carved such beautiful and creative pumpkins.

This Halloween I was driving down a busy street in Cleveland, Ohio trying to remember directions to my next house call when I spotted a small white furry thing running in and out of the street. I pulled over, stopped my truck, and left it running in the curb lane of the street. I began chasing that small white furry object in and out of store fronts and under cars for a few blocks when I finally caught that little kitten. He was actually gray and white. No mother or owner was in sight, so I held him close to me, retrieved my truck, and proceeded to complete my last house call. I told him he was going to get hit by a car running around like that and we really couldn't have that! The little guy may not have known who I was- and was to become - but he clung to me as tightly as he could.

They were never surprised when I found another animal to bring home. He was frightened at first, but when he warmed up - WOW- was he a handful. He ran from room to room looking for the next item of paper, cloth, toys, or anything he could play with. When I sat on the floor playing board games with my step daughter, he would run up to me, place his paws on my shoulder, and hit me over and over. Cutest thing ever. I named him Dynamite. It fit him.

When he grew, he followed me everywhere. Each day I walked the dogs he came along. He acted more like a dog than a cat. This was fine when we walked together, but when I needed to go to the barn I was afraid he could be injured by one of the young horses I was training. To avoid him seeing me, I would sneak out the front door and walk around the block to the barn.

I think of Dynamite each Halloween and how he came to be mine. It is a great time of year, but I always encourage my pet owners to protect their black cats at this time of year. Most owners know this.

Write your story here_____

Cutest Halloween Costume

Halloween is a fun time.

Hi, my name is Kitty. Halloween is almost here. I am trying on the costume my owners bought for me to wear on that special night. How do you like it? They said they mulled over dozens of choices before deciding on this adorable get up. I think it suits me just fine. The truth is deep down inside I am an angel, my family said so.

The family is ready for the spooky holiday. The decorations are all set, the candy bowls have been taken from their stored places, and they talk of all the tricks and treats they are planning for the young trick-or-theaters. I and the dog are not allowed chocolate- oh darn - but we like treats too. We try to avoid the tricks but are ready to do anything for the treats. My favorite treats are salmon or chicken flavored goodies. Dog is hoping for treats too- he likes everything, but dog bones seem appropriate for this Halloween celebration.

Dog is dressing up and going house to house with the children. I will be sitting here waiting for everyone to come my way. Please bring treats if you are coming to our house. And don't forget ...

Share your stories about Halloween - all about your pets' favorite treats and pictures of the costumes you have for your pets.

Write your story here

His Little Teddy Bear Costume

Hi, I'm the dog. I am ready for the big night. You heard from Kitty last week and saw her costume. I considered going trick or treating as a ghost or a vampire or Freddie Krueger, but my owners decided I am their little teddy bear, so this is what they chose for me. What do you think?

Everyone in the house thinks I am so cute and they want to kiss me over and over.

I'm going house to house with the children and will accept any and all appropriate treats. I am not allowed chocolate, but dog bones are much appreciated. I would love to see how your owner dressed you this Halloween. Mom said she saw many pet owners fitting their pets with costumes at the local pet stores. One woman had an alligator costume. Wow! That dog is going to scare everyone. Others included Superman, turtles, McDonald's food costumes and I'll bet you have thought of others.

Hope all you folks like the decorations in the neighborhood- the pumpkins, corn stalks, ghosts, lights, and some of the gruesome additions to the yard decor. Hope it's not too cold and you get lots and lots of treats and the tricks are fun. Keep us posted.

Stay safe and watch over the children. Kitty is staying home, so visit her for your treats at our house.

Share your Halloween costumes and your great Halloween adventures.

Write your story here____

A Season for Giving Thanks

I graduated from High School when I was 16 years old. I started teaching nursery school children during the day at my church and attending night school at the community college two streets from my home. I was a biology major. I had no actual plan, but I had a dream. I wanted to be a doctor.

My first college class was general biology. Everyone in class worked during the day like I did.

They had dreams too. I was naturally shy, but because everyone seemed to understand me, we all became friends. One man in particular and I talked about our plans. Since starting night classes, I deviated slightly from my original plans. I pursued a career as an ambulance driver. I told my friend about this and how my friends and family wanted me to study nursing, but I still wanted to be a doctor. He said, "Don't stop at being an ambulance driver, and don't stop at being a nurse, go all the way to being a doctor. You can do it.' His words encouraged me for all the years I studied. I am thankful to have had such a great friend.

My family left Ohio and my Grandfather allowed me to live with him. He was patient and kind and allowed me the freedom to attend my college classes and work when I was able. He took care of me and protected me for many years. I was able to attend nursing school at a large hospital near our home. After graduating from nursing school, I pursued a career in veterinary medicine. It was because of his care I was able to do so.

My Grandfather was an immigrant and only had an eighth grade education, but he was the smartest man I have ever known. He supported all my educational endeavors. After attending graduation from veterinary school, he told me how proud he was of me. He told me it took a lot of courage to do what I did, but it was only possible because of him. I think it took a lot of courage for his family to come to this country and for him to roll steel every day for many years and raise a family and take care of the people he loved. I am thankful beyond any words to express how much to this man – my Grandfather - who taught me everything about courage and doing the right thing and always taking care of family.

Over the past years, my Father and Mother have helped me in many ways. They gave me a home in a foreign state, helped me find gainful employment, pay off all my bills, and have the courage to find a new life enjoying the ocean, rivers, manatees, pelicans, sea turtles, family and many more things. I am truly grateful.

Friends and family always make a difference.

Write your story here

Otters and Bass and Alligators

My brother inspired my love for kayaking along the spring fed rivers in Florida. When I visited him and his wife, I was determined to see manatees. Unfortunately, the manatees only come into the springs when the ocean waters they live in become cold in winter months. The manatees seek the warmer water in the springs because the constant temperature there is 72 degrees Fahrenheit- much warmer than the ocean. For many years I was either too early or too late to see manatees, but never seemed to miss the gators.

One visit my brother and his wife and I canoed Alexander Springs. While cruising the river my brother fished and caught three bass. As he admired his catch, other river travelers passed and told us there was a gator up the way with babies sitting on her back. This I wanted to see. My brother agreed.

He tied the bass to a tree along the river with shoe laces. Pretty ingenious. The three of us continued along the river and spotted the mother gator with many little babies on her back. Usually I am terrified of gators, but thought this was great! I took pictures and 'oozed' and 'abashed' and acted like a complete tourist that just arrived in Florida.

When we returned to retrieve the bass, suddenly my brother jumped out of the canoe and swam to his fish. Thieving otters were trying to steal his bass. They must have thought "WHAT AN EASY CATCH TODAY!" My brother, however, had no intentions of allowing those fish to be apprehended by those otters. He was fearless and unconcerned that the otters could present a problem or even bite him. He retrieved his bass, we finished our canoeing, and he tells the story of how he almost lost his bass because I wanted to see some gator babies on their mother's back.

It was a great day on the river.

Write your story here_____

Baby Gorillas

During my last year in veterinary school I chose rotations that allowed me to ride with the zoo veterinarian. The Columbus, Ohio zoo had 2 baby twin gorillas. We were taught that it was not advisable to touch the gorillas due to the possibility of disease transmission, but the temptation was more than I could bear.

One day I stood outside the twin gorilla's pen and watched as they delighted in swinging around the tree branches and patting their chests. They would stop and look at me to make sure I was still watching them- and I was. They played for a while, then one of them came to the front of the cage and put his arm through the bars stretching as much as he could trying to reach his little hand my way. Priceless. I wanted to reach out and grab that little hand. I did not see cameras, but am certain they were around that enclosure. I imagined bells and whistles going off if I dared touch that little guy. I did not touch him or his twin, but I wanted to.

On another trip to the zoo, I learned the zoo employees wanted to repair a broken structure in the outdoor exhibit of the gorillas. The females were inside, but the males refused to come in. When the zoo veterinarian and the few students with him (I was one of them) stepped out of the truck, the male gorillas began running full speed into the indoor enclosure. We laughed stating, "Doc, it looks like they know you." He had his tranquilizer gun in hand and, indeed, they did know him- even from the distance we were away from them.

I was told that when the veterinarian shoots the tranquilizer into the gorilla, they must be very careful because the gorilla is able to pick the syringe off their body. They throw it back at the veterinarian. This can be dangerous because the medications used to tranquilize the gorilla are very powerful and can cause harm and even death to a human. We found it amusing they were intelligent enough to do this. Then, as we were told the gorillas throw the darts back at the veterinarian, we were told they hand the syringe to their caregivers. "Awe," we said, we wished we were their caregivers instead of their veterinarians.

Write your story here_____

I Just Wanted to Ride

Like many girls, I have always loved horses. When I was a young girl, my mother arranged for me to work at a horse farm on Saturdays in exchange for time riding. When I started working on the farm, the owner was home and directed my work. When I finished, she chose a safe horse for me to ride in a small riding ring near her barn. These were treasured memories and the riding thrilled me beyond words.

One Saturday, she was away at a horse show. I cleaned all twenty stalls in the barn - a huge accomplishment for a young girl. There were llamas in one stall and when I opened the door to clean their stall, they rushed past me and ran out of the stall into the horse pasture. I knew I needed to return them to their stall, so without thinking, I opened the pasture gate to herd them out of the pasture. This was a bad plan. Not only did the llamas come, seeing the open gate, the horses stampeded past me running into and through the barn to a field behind the barn. They were free and I could not stop them. What a disaster!

I had no idea what to do. I thought I lost all the horses. How would I explain this? Then, suddenly, they turned and headed back to the barn. Later I learned this is a usual behavior for horses to stay where they are fed. Happy to have them return, most ran back into the pasture. A few horses ran into stalls in the barn. I was able to return them to the pasture easily. The disaster that started with the llamas escaping ended with them returning to their stall.

When the owner came home, there was no trace of the trouble I had, however, she was amazed at the work I had done. She knew how much work went into cleaning all those stalls, but it didn't seem like work to me. I was in heaven being around the horses all day and looking forward to a few minutes in the saddle. To tell the truth, I would have done twice the number of stalls to ride. She called my mother and made arrangements for me to spend the night because she had a surprise for me.

I was excited thinking of which horse she would choose for me to ride and how fun it would be to be to walk and trot in the small arena, but the surprise had nothing to do with riding. She took me to a car race. All I can remember is how bored I was sitting in the bleacher seats alone shivering, eating a candy bar, and watching those cars drive around and around the track. My mother never took me to her barn again, but eventually I owned my own horses and was able to ride any time I wanted.

Write your story here____

No Ordinary Day at the Laundromat

    I agree, sometimes life is about little things. Two little things I have always wished for are a washer and dryer at home.

    Until that dream comes true, I appreciate commercial washers and dryers at local laundromats. Since I try to see the glass as half full and the up side of things when able, I see the laundromat as a great asset. When I go, I am able to wash and dry many loads at one time. There have been occasions I felt like I was the luckiest person alive - not because I won the lottery or made a great invention of some kind - but because I was the only one at the laundromat and used almost all the washers. Funny what one can consider a good day and luck.

Once, while working, I decided to wash clothes at a nearby Laundromat at lunch time. This meant more of the glass half full concept - lunch, wash, and all my loads done at the same time. Didn't think life could get much better. I started my loads as usual. Soon after I arrived, two men arrived. One was an older gentleman and the other a grown man, but younger.

While we waited for washers and dryers to finish, I overheard the conversation between the two men. The younger man repeatedly asked the same questions. When would they be done? Would they have supper after they were finished? What were all the people doing shopping at the stores near the laundromat? And more. The younger man also stated the obvious over and over- they were doing wash and would be done soon, but how soon? Each time the younger man spoke, the older man kindly and softly responded and assured him they would done with the wash soon as well as answer the same question for the tenth time as if it were the first time being asked.

This went on the entire time we washed clothes together. I was touched by the kindness and patience of the older man. I was sure this young man was a permanent part of his life and he never seemed annoyed and never spoke harshly to him. I thought how easily annoyed I am sometimes.

When I was finished my wash, I walked over to the older gentleman and said, "You are a really kind man. It has been very touching to watch you with him." In a surprised voice, the man replied, "Why, thank you." - as if he considered his acts of patience, kindness and love to this younger man just normal, not extraordinary, the way I thought. His kindness and patience inspire me to be more like him.

Write your story here___

The Art of Naming a Pet

I am amused at the names my clients give the family pets. From Fizzgig to Gator, many have favorite characters or family members they name their pet after.

We adopted a little tiger cat who was a terror from the moment she came into our home. She raced everywhere in the house, darted under furniture, climbed draperies, and jumped from counters to cabinets to the floor. She was exhausting.

My step daughter loved cats and this kitten was her favorite.

When we named her, I asked my step daughter what name she wanted for this kitten. We both agreed she was a monster. We thought about naming her Monster. Then, my step daughter thought more and she said, 'Well, I really like the name Donna.'

We considered our options. Should we name her Monster or Donna? We went back and forth and still couldn't decide. Then she said, 'Well, I also like the name Lisa.'

What to do? Now we had three names to choose. Should she be Monster, Donna, or Lisa? Since we couldn't decide, we did the only logical thing, we named her Monster Donna Lisa. When you said this about 100 times, it sounded like a real name anyone might name their pet. I am certain there are NO other cats in the world named Monster Donna Lisa, but there are many unique other names as well as the usual names like Bella and Max and Tiger, and others.

Write your story here

Solomon's Injury

When I wanted to train Solomon to jump, I wanted to use small wooden structures called cavallettis. These long wooden poles attach to wood in the shape of an 'X' at both ends. This allows the pole to be set low, or a little higher, and even one more measure higher if the 'X' is rotated to change the level of the bar. Cavalletti is used for training to jump as well as for helping horses become flexible and conditioned.

I have great friends who knew my love for horses. When I told them I wanted cavallettis, they made 6 of them for me. I treasured those wooden poles and took them wherever Sol and I moved to. They were a great help for us as we learned dressage and jumping. The same friends helped in another time of need.

One evening when I was trying to load Solomon into a trailer, he refused to go in. A man helping me pulled firmly on his lead rope which made Solomon pull back. As he pulled back, his head went up and the man let go of the lead rope. Sol's whole body went into the air - he went up so high he went over backwards. When he landed, he struck the bones at the base of his neck against a concrete parking block in the driveway.

My precious horse was hurt. For a few moments I wondered if he was alive. I heard stories about horses striking the top of their head - known as the poll- and not surviving the injury. When he stood, the muscles of his shoulders and back tensed. I called my friends and a local veterinarian. They came immediately. The veterinarian administered medication and took x-rays. Sol broke bones called the withers at the base of his neck. These bones are not back bones, but boney projections that extend from the back bones.

I couldn't leave him so I pulled my car into the barn isle and spent the night. During the night, I was awakened by a loud snorting/snoring sound. I jumped out of my car and ran into Solomon's stall to find him lying quietly there. He looked up at me as if to say, 'What's wrong, mom?'

I stood for a moment and the loud snorting came again. It was the horse in the next stall. Relieved, I went back to sleep. The next day my friends drove me and Solomon to the Veterinary Hospital hours from our homes. They knew I was too upset to drive my horse myself. The veterinarian there assured me Solomon would heal and be fine. His bones healed and we rode again and again and again.

Write your story here_____

The most beautiful of them all

When I first came to Florida, everything was new and exciting fabulous. After years of being here it is all still exciting and fabulous.

There are scary things like poisonous snakes- coral snakes, rattlesnakes, and others - along with alligators and bears, but there are also sweet little critters. During one visit to a local spring and walking on a boardwalk, mom and I spotted an Armadillo rooting around in the leaves. As he made his way towards us, he looked up at everyone looking down at him, seemed to wonder what we all were looking at, then nonchalantly proceeded to continue his quest to find bugs and other meal items in the ground and surrounding foliage. I thought he was darling. He was not as enamored with us as we were with him.

Turtles are another of my favorites of the day. I have watched gopher turtles come in and out of their holes as well as rescued babies off streets. I also love painted turtles sunning themselves on logs and rocks. Once I rescued an alligator snapper from the dangers of the road. He was quite quick at snapping my shoe when it was close to his mouth. I was wise enough to keep my fingers away. While kayaking in a spring run near Gainesville, I spotted a baby turtle- he was about the size of a silver dollar. Cutest little guy. I wanted a picture, so I pulled my kayak close- he darted under water because he had no idea I am the nicest person and would never dream of hurting him. He periodically surfaced to see if I was still close. When he saw me, he immediately withdrew back under the water. Even with constant assurances from me, he refused to allow me to take a photo. Sea turtles hatching and running to the ocean are also my favorites. I guess I have many favorites.

We see eagles everywhere. One day I saw one land on Daytona Beach. Others suggested I had seen an Osprey. I was certain it was an eagle. The all white head and feathers on his legs that looked like trousers and a stance that is unique to the eagle- like he means business- are all clues I had spotted an eagle. Gorgeous is a word for these creatures. One bird rescue in a town around Orlando has eagles as well. One of their eagles was found as an orphan who was 1 day old when found out of the nest. They raised him and cannot turn him safely to the wild, so they care for him. We have the wonderful opportunity to visit this beautiful guy.

Pelicans arrive each day at the ocean to fish for breakfast. They glide in the sky and over the waves. When they spot an enticing meal, they dive directly into the water. I could watch them all day. When visiting the Florida Keys, we stay at a campground that has pelicans close. They wait for us and other campers to bring our fish for cleaning in hopes for an easy meal.

But my all time favorites are the manatees. I visited Florida for years trying to get a look at one in person. Finally, I have seen them up close and personal. In fact, one morning mom and I walked over to the spring near our home- the fountain of youth, as Ponce Deleon described the springs in Florida. While standing on the boat dock, a family of manatees came close- a male, female, and baby. What an unbelievable treat. Right in front of us- a reach out and touch moment. The gentle sea cows are social and beautiful. I understand it is a federal offense to touch them, but some things can be very difficult to resist. These are memories for a lifetime.

Share your story of fabulous moments.

Write your story here

Cover Girl Mattie

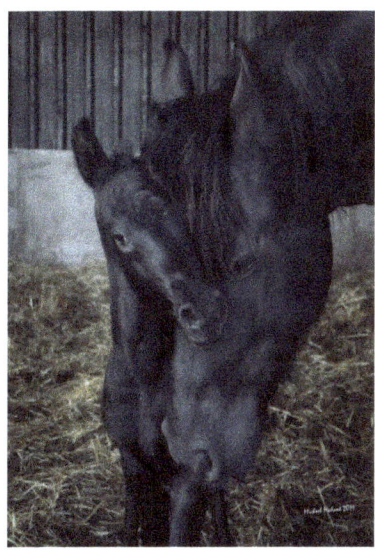

We bought Cover Girl Mattie as a yearling. Like her name, she was beautiful. We broke her and trained her to race. She won many races and survived a racing accident. When she retired, she became a mommy.

Mattie's first baby came into the world with slight difficulty. In veterinary school we were taught that a foal should be delivered with their nose coming in between their two front feet/legs. We were taught that any abnormal presentation needed correction and that correction was accomplished by pushing the foal back into the mother's uterus, correcting the incorrect position, and then having the baby delivered correctly. In about two seconds I learned that this is easier said than done.

I arrived home at 12:30am after working as a nurse to find Mattie's baby coming with ONE leg and his nose. I called some local farmers because everyone knows it is critical to deliver a foal quickly and if there are problems, they need addressed or mom and/or baby could be lost.

I tried to push that foal back to correct the position, but when I couldn't, I placed my hand inside Mattie and determined that the foal's right front leg was back, but had enough room to be delivered. I began pulling the foal's left front leg and the mouth. This was difficult because foals are wet and slippery. Mattie strained to push as I pulled. I put my foot on the back of her rear leg to use this as leverage to pull more on the foal. I yelled, "Push, Mattie" as she continued to push and I continued to pull.

We worked for what seemed like an eternity but was probably 10-15 minutes. Finally, that foal plopped out onto the straw bedding in the stall. He looked exactly like his mommy- a huge black boy with long spindly legs. As I admired him, Mattie fell to the ground. I couldn't move. I began crying and asked the farmers who had arrived to help if she died. The memories of mamas that ruptured blood vessels and died during foaling filled my thoughts. As a veterinarian, I should have checked her, but as her owner and mama, I was too upset and afraid to. With calm voices, they assured me she was just exhausted.

After a short rest, Mattie stood up. She instinctively knew she had to have this little guy nurse. The first milk is important for the babies because it provides proteins that protect against disease. Both Mattie and her foal were unsteady on their feet. I helped this little guy into position to nurse. She nuzzled him as if to say, 'Hello, son, I am your mommy.' I watched Mattie love her first little boy.

The next day I realized the foal injured a nerve in his right front leg when it was not in the correct position coming through the birth canal. I called another veterinarian who he assured me the nerve was most likely bruised and would heal without complication. He was right and the foal healed within 5 days without any treatment from me.

He ran in the pasture as if nothing ever went wrong with his welcome into this world. He bounced off his mother and when he ran one direction, she followed as quickly as she could to keep up with the little guy. He wore her out. Most moms know how this is with their little ones. He was fast. He was born to race.

Write your story here

The Putters

I worked as a home health nurse for children. Every child I cared for was precious to me, but one particular young man had a special place in my heart. He lived with his grandmother and father and uncles.

I cared for him at night time when his family slept. I brought soda, donuts, and movies for us to enjoy until wee hours of the mornings. We played checkers and other board games on the floor of his bedroom.

He was wheelchair bound, so when we would go places together during the day, I would pick him up, transfer him to the car, and put the wheelchair in the trunk. Everything is portable. We went to movies and stores. One day we decided to go to a fun park called "Swings and Things."

There were go carts, bumper boats, and putt putt golf.

He was unable to push the gas pedal in the go carts and I was unable to sit with him in the small cart, but we had a blast in the bumper boats. I carried him into the boat- a small rubber sea craft in a little pool- and sat next to him- holding him safely the entire time. As my step daughter 'bumped' into us in another boat, this little boy would throw his head back and laugh as his belly shook.

After the bumper boats, I placed him in his wheelchair, and we headed to the putting greens. I have never been a fan of golf, but am a great lover of putt putt. As we made our way through each of the greens, I noticed that when this young man putted, my step daughter blocked his putt with her putter- she placed her putter in front of the hole preventing his ball from going into the hole. I was astounded, I said, 'You do realize he's in a wheelchair?' She didn't care, she kept doing it.

Then when she putted, he wheeled closely to the hole and blocked her putt with his putter. I was exasperated. I said, 'You both are terrible, I have some news, we are NOT keeping score any longer. If you each have to win so badly you do this to each other, we will not keep score.' They stopped sabotaging each others' putts and we had fun finishing putting. In the end, I was glad she never seemed to see the wheelchair, she just treated him like a regular boy. He appreciated that.

Write your story here

Henny Penny and Cock-a-Doodle

I wanted fresh eggs every morning. Obviously, the only way to have this is to have a chicken. But where to get a chicken?

One of my favorite clients knew where to get chickens. He hatched eggs and seemed to know everything you could imagine about chickens, ducks, geese, and many other birds. I shared my problem with him and, since he was going to an auction where chickens were sold, he offered to buy a chicken for me.

When he brought me my chicken, he brought what he called 6 chickens and one rooster. He said a rooster among the chickens helps the egg laying process. What did I know? As an unexpected surprise, he thought I would like a little Bantam hen and rooster. They were tiny and cute. I took them and instantly fell in love. I named her Henny Penny after children's stories I read, and him Cock a Doodle-for obvious reasons.

Having cats that were bigger than the Bantams presented a problem. The cats treated the Bantams like toys. When attacked by the cats, they ran and flew to me. Sometimes they flew on the backs of the horses. Surprisingly, the horses did not mind them on their backs. I scooped them up and held them safely from the cats. It was obvious these two little ones were someone's pets and hand raised.

One day we could not find Cock a Doodle. We thought the worst happened. I left for work sad to say good – bye to him. Later that evening, my friend called to tell me he was working in the vegetable garden and suddenly he heard a cock a doodle doo and turned to see that little rooster strutting his way. He was fine and had been hiding from the cats.

There's amazing math involved in chicken procreation. These two little birds had many little Henny's and little Doodle's. Eventually I had 30 chickens and roosters.

Also, the six chickens and one rooster I was supposed to have received turned out to be six roosters and one chicken. She did lay wonderful and delicious eggs, but the boys did not stay, they fight. So much for someone knowing the difference between chickens and roosters at that young age. It can be challenging.

Write your story here_____

The Miracle of the Little Chickens

My little Bantam hen, Henny Penny had so many chicks she should have been a rabbit. Each time she laid eggs, she hid them and faithfully sat on them for 21 days -the length of time it takes to hatch chicks.

Chicks growing in eggs are amazing. The egg yolk is actually an 'egg' made in the ovary of the hen. The egg leaves the ovary and as it travels down tubules, it is covered with the 'egg white'- which is made of a protein called albumin. As the egg contents continue to travel down the tubules, a shell made from calcium is added just before the hen lays the egg.

When an egg is fertilized, a chick grows inside the egg. The chick uses the yolk as food to grow. Oxygen and carbon dioxide are exchanged through the shell. Over the 21 days the chick is growing, it fills the whole inside of the egg. All the parts of the chick grow as well as the down feathers. When it time comes to hatch, the chick uses its beak to break a hole in the shell. It continues to chip away at the egg shell until it is free from the shell. The chicks chirped the entire time they were hatching - seemingly telling the world there were coming out of those eggs.

When the chick came out, I loved watching them- their little beaks, little faces, little eyes, little wings, down feathers, and their tiny little feet. The minute they were hatched they ran and chased after their mom. They hid in the wings and feathers of their mom and sometimes their dad as they grew to have little chicks of their own.

The miracle of birth. Einstein said either everything is a miracle or nothing is a miracle. I think everything is a miracle.

Write your story here_____

Harvey

I found my cocker spaniel pup, Harvey, in Amish country. Unfortunately, he was never vaccinated. I am usually careful to avoid exposing young pups to older dogs or dogs that are not well until the pup is older and vaccinated, however, it was a busy time in my life. When Harvey came to work with me at a local veterinary clinic, he became ill with parvo virus.

I first learned of the devastating disease of parvo in dogs in the early 80's when the virus was first identified. Vaccines were quickly created and decreased the incidence of the disease as well as decreased the loss of pets.

Parvo is a virus that infects the cells in the intestinal tract of a dog. This causes severe diarrhea with blood, vomiting, and loss of appetite. The intestinal damage is devastating in itself, however, parvo is a virus that attacks and lowers the white blood cells in a dog's body. Since white blood cells are the cells that help fight infection, dogs with parvo are at risk for serious infections- such as pneumonia or sepsis (infection in the blood). These infections are the usual reason pets infected with parvo virus are lost. Parvo virus may also attack a young pup's heart. When this happens, there is no treatment for the injury to the heart.

Harvey became sick. I was worried. Harvey not only had diarrhea, his pooh was pure blood. I started his therapy- IV's and antibiotics as well as medication to stop the vomiting- which is usually not effective. Harvey battled parvo for 8 days. He had an IV in one front leg for 4 days and then the other leg for the next 4 days. He held his little leg out and let the fluids go into his body. I watched him day and night. I placed an IV pole by my bed, placed plastic on the bed to prevent soiling, and shined my flashlight at the fluid bag to make certain the IV's dripped all night. For days, Harvey sat on the side of the bed heaving and vomiting.

He was sick so long I did not think he would survive, but after 8 days, he stopped vomiting, his stool improved, and he began eating. There were no obvious indications of damage to his intestines or heart after he recovered. He played and enjoyed a normal life. He beat the odds.

I have treated many pets for parvo virus infection. Some are happy endings like Harvey and some endings are heartbreaking for owners. I always advise owners Ito vaccinate all pups. Even with controversy over vaccines, it is the best way to prevent this major disease in dogs.

Write your story here

Samantha

My first dog was a Doberman pinscher – German shepherd mix. My family was offered this 'male' dog and my parents said yes. We excitedly decided to name 'him' Sam.

When Sam arrived, we discovered 'he' was a 'she.' We decided to keep her name, but call her Samantha- Sam for short.

She was instantly part of the family. I played in the yard with her – teaching her to fetch, sit, stay, run squirrels up trees and poles, and knew the joy of owning a dog. Mom used her to babysit the younger children. She accompanied my brothers to the woods near our home daily. One of her best talents was to hide quietly under the table at dinner time. This came in handy when mom made liver. We hated liver, Sam loved liver. When mom wasn't looking, Sam took care of business and never told on us. Everyone was a winner.

One day Sam became mopey and would not eat. My parents took her to a veterinarian. I heard the word "distemper." Distemper is a disease in dogs caused by a virus that attacks the intestines of affected animals and causes vomiting, diarrhea, not wanting to eat, and being very sick. The distemper virus can travel to the brain. When this happens, seizures may develop and there is very little chance the dog will survive.

I was worried and, when I am worried, I cry. We forced Sam to eat by using a turkey baster to give her baby cereal. After about a week, she began to recover and was herself again. Dogs may become ill after exposure to other dogs with this virus or other animals such as raccoons carrying the virus.

There is a vaccine available to dog owners to prevent distemper. Vaccinating is the best method of preventing the major diseases in dogs. In addition to distemper, vaccines are available for rabies, hepatitis, leptospirosis, kennel cough, and parvo. After seeing the devastating effects of disease in the dogs I loved, I am a believer in vaccines. I have vaccinated every dog, cat, horse, and goat since that time.

Write your story here_____

Alex

I found another pup to add to the family- a Sheltie I named Alex. It always amazes me how fast one can fall in love with a little guy -I estimate about 2.7 seconds or less.

One afternoon, when Alex was young, we gardened together. He walked in and out of the flower beds as I tried to plant and fertilize. While focusing on the flowers, I lost track of Alex. When I discovered he wasn't with me, I frantically shouted his name and searched the yard. I checked everywhere- including the street in front of our home and the roads into the grounds where we lived, but did not find him.

With my mind racing and my heart pounding, I started up the porch steps to phone for help. Suddenly, I stopped half way up the steps because there, sitting at the top of the steps, wagging his tail, sat my Alex. As I scooped him up in my arms and kissed his little face, I told him how worried I was and how happy I was that he was not lost after all. I told him how he scared his mommy. I should have known- already having a Sheltie - that Shelties never leave you. Where you are, they are.

When Alex was about 3 years old, he developed a stone in his bladder from minerals in his diet. I surgically removed it; however, the condition went unnoticed for a while. When he appeared to be passing urine, very little or none came out due to the stone obstructing the flow of urine. I believe the blockage injured his kidneys because when Alex was about 7 years old, his kidneys began to fail to do their job.

In human medicine, patients are offered dialysis to filter their blood when their kidneys are not doing so. This may be available now at specialty clinics, but was not well developed when Alex's kidneys failed to do their job. Alex accompanied me everywhere so I could give him medications and fluids as needed as well as being near me comforted him. I was committed to racing and training horses at the racetrack 2-3 times a week and was aware that taking a dog into the racetrack could result in a $250.00 fine, but I couldn't leave him at home.

When we went into the race track, Alex rested on the passenger seat beside me out of view. But, when I took my race horse from the prep barn to the track, I saw Alex sitting in the driver's seat looking out the window. As I passed I said, "Alex, you're blowing our cover. Everyone can see you." Luckily, no one seemed to notice and we were never fined.

Even after several months of diligent care, and trying to figure a way to help Alex, the day came I could see that we were not on the winning side of Alex's kidney disease. It was one of the saddest days of my life to say good- bye to that wonderful little dog. When these beautiful creatures come into our lives they bring happiness and love and time seems to fly by until that dreadful day. Saying good-bye is always heartbreaking.

Some say it's part of the deal. The more you love something or someone, the more it hurts to say good- bye. The only other option is to not love- and that is not an option I wish to choose. I will always have memories of Alex to make me happy for the time we had together.

Write your story here___

The Debate

If I could write another caption for this photo, it would read, "Where ya been?" -as our pets sit, waiting for us to come over to other side.

Do animals go to heaven? I do not profess to know the absolute answer to this question, but I have opinions and I think there is a heaven and think animals go there. I think I am not alone in my thinking.

In defense of my argument, I am a believer in the Bible and God put more animals on the Ark than He did people. Also, animals are indisputably some of His greatest creations. They have life and love with their whole hearts and being.

There are so many amazing creatures - the colorful birds, elephants, giraffes, zebras, horses, whales, manatees, sea turtles, and of course, our beloved cats and dogs. What would heaven (if you believe in heaven as I do) be like without them? They are here, why wouldn't they be there?

I often share a story with my clients that goes something like this- One day, while watching TV, a TV host shared a story of a little boy who seemed sad on his show. He asked the boy, "Why so sad."

The little boy said, "My dog just died."

The host said sympathetically, "Well, doesn't it help to know he's in heaven with God?"

The little boy looked up at him with a puzzled face and asked, "What would God want with a dead dog?"

We laugh. Apparently, the concept of life after this life for his dog apparently evaded this young man, but the question still remains, 'do all dogs really go to heaven?' My vote is 'yes.' We will all find out one day.

Write your story here____

Millie Millie

Millie was Angel's baby. Angel was no angel, but, her terrific breeding made her a great race horse. Millie inherited her mom's sour disposition, but she also inherited her racing talent. To help her be manageable, I spent time handling her and playing with her beginning after her birth.

Since mother horses can be protective and dangerous, I tied Angel when I entered her stall to play with Millie. Then, I chased Millie around the stall and under her mother until I caught her. Daily I rubbed her entire body, picked up her feet and tapped her hooves, and held her to train her to stop struggling. In preparation for placing a harness on her, I lifted her tail and placed my arm under it where the tail piece of the harness sits. I brushed her and played with her- always talking to her. After a while, she trusted me. Even the toughest girls can be won over by love and patience.

When Millie was a yearling, it was time to train her to the equipment so she could train and race. My partner made the first attempt at putting a harness on her. Millie exploded and kicked at him. I took the harness, walked up to her, and put it on her - the tail piece as well as the girth around her belly and the chest pieces. She never fussed for me. I think it was because I was her human mommy and the trust that developed between us was a great asset.

Millie did everything I asked her to. She broke to the equipment and cart with ease. She trained well and raced like the wind. One day she became ill with a condition I never saw before and still don't know what it was. She seemed to have pain in her abdomen like a horse with colic, but all the horses I treated for this improved in a day or so. It took five days for Millie to recover. She wanted to lie down and roll and I couldn't let her because when horses roll, they are in danger of twisting their intestines. If she twisted her intestines, she would not survive and surgery to untwist them was not an option for us.

I watched her day and night for five long days. When she was quiet and resting peacefully in her stall, I wrapped her lead rope around my leg and slept for short periods on the floor of the barn outside her stall. I did this so when she began to thrash, she pulled the rope around my leg, waking me. When she was restless, I kept her on her feet - which can be challenging with a 1,100 pound animal, medicated her for pain, and walked her for hours. After those five tortuous days Millie and I weathered together, thankfully she recovered and raced for many years.

I once thought horses did not form bonds with their humans like dogs and cats, but one night, when I arrived home from work, I turned on the lights in the barn and discovered Millie and another horse opened their stall doors and were loose. This is a concern because horses can be injured or killed on roads if hit by cars or trucks. As I entered the barn, Millie and the other horse casually walked into the back door of the barn and came to me as if to ask, "Where you been, mom?" I patted their necks and returned them to their stalls - safe and sound. My trainer once told me the horse knows the person who feeds them and the person who plays with them. I was both and they were my girls.

My horses were my pets first and my racing girls second.

Share a story.

Write your story here_____

Isaiah and Solomon's Adventures

My Solomon was a great horse to raise my young Isaiah because he was kind and gentle and patient. Isaiah was a Trakehner - a German warm blood- that came to me and Sol as a yearling weighing 1,200 pounds, but grew to 2,600 pounds. Solomon was a Thoroughbred who weighed 1,100 pounds. Sol was senior to Isaiah when he arrived, so Sol was boss. They were best friends and Isaiah followed Solomon everywhere- which would normally be a great thing because Sol usually never misbehaved.

Such was not the case on a few occasions. Once, the two of them escaped from a pasture on a farm we were boarding at. Sol found it great fun to run away from me while Isaiah raced right behind him. The problem was that there was danger in the road close by and I did not want them to just run free. I tried everything to get the two horses to come to me - I called them, shook a can of grain at them, and tried to cut them off from running away from me. Sol darted past me every time I was close and Isaiah ran after him. Nothing I did mattered.

Finally, Isaiah stopped and looked at me with his big baby eyes as if to say, "Sol, it's mommy, why are we running?" And then he came to me. After Isaiah was apprehended, Sol reluctantly followed. It seemed Sol liked being the 'bad horse' - getting them both in the dog house.

Another winter day, I put the two of them in a pasture and left to work 30 miles away. When I returned, I saw footprints in the snow from the pasture, all over the front and back yards, and leading into the street. The owner of the farm told me what a terrible time she had with my two boys while I was away. She chased them for an hour and fell in the snow hurting her back. First, they ran her around the yards, then up and down the busy street in front of her farm before she safely returned them to their stalls. I wish they could have told me all about their adventure, but they remained silent. Their innocent faces hid all the mischief they had gotten into. I never left them out again unless I could watch them. My two banditos.

Write your story here_____

Isaiah

I have a treasured friend who trained me to ride. Since I was a working student, and could not afford my Thoroughbred, Sol, to stay at her barn, he stayed at a barn up the road. We made arrangements for lessons and I put Sol's equipment on and walked him down the road to her farm.

It was my first lesson and I was running late, so, as I walked up the road, I rehearsed what I would say. When I arrived at her barn, I apologized for being 15 minutes late, but said I would pay for an hour if she was willing to give me 45 minutes of instruction.

She then stood straighter and firmly said, "15 minutes! You are an HOUR and 15 minutes late and I do not have time to be messing with you." I don't remember any other words because I was stunned and stood motionless. Everything was a blur as thoughts churned in my mind- we moved 20 miles to the opposite side of town to learn with her, I traveled every day to this new area to ride, my heart felt broken at the thought of not riding with her because I was so excited to, and I had just walked my horse down the road. I tried to think of how I could make such a mistake.

I was speechless. After scolding me, it seemed she realized I had no idea I was this late. I wasn't leaving. Finally, she agreed to give me a lesson. She gave me an hour of instruction. She liked us. We became very good friends. I was never late again. It is customary and respectful for a rider to dress in riding pants and riding boots, but my student budget did not allow me to have these luxury items at that time in life. I wore corduroy jeans and attached my spurs to running shoes. She was a proper woman and a professional trainer, but she never mentioned my dress. She understood. We trained in dressage work together many years. She made me a rider. I am forever grateful.

When I visited her several years later, she had a yearling Trakehner for sale. When he trotted across the pasture, he looked like he was floating on air. I told her I wanted him. I named him Isaiah. My trainer once said the horse does the best for the person who breaks and trains them. I was determined to be that person for Isaiah.

Isaiah was a stallion when I bought him, but

after dragging me across a field to chase some mares, I made arrangements to castrate him. Problem solved. When the time came to teach him to ride, the process was easy because he trusted me. He was 17.2 hands tall- almost 6 feet tall) and weighed 2,600 pounds. It took me a year to adjust to his large size. Sometimes I stood on my truck bumper or the wheel of the tractor to pull myself onto his back. He always stood patiently and motionless.

When we first started riding we just walked and trotted. One day he began to canter slowly. It was amazing, but his stride was so huge, I rolled right out of the saddle and landed on the ground. That boy stopped and looked down at me with his big, beautiful eyes as if to ask, "What're you doing down there, mom?"

Isaiah jumped, did dressage, and rode trails. I rode him everywhere. We rode English, Western, and bareback. I have the best memories of the 17 years we shared together.

Write your story here____

Friendship Because Life is Hard

My Aunt's name was Mildred. Some called her Millie. As children, we couldn't say Mildred or Millie, so we called her Aunt Moddy. She was young at heart and drove a red Mustang. She told fascinating stories of giving children free ice cream cones when she worked at an ice cream stand. We never knew if her stories were true, but we loved hearing them.

Aunt Moddy filled our lives with laughter and fun, but when she was older, she became sick with cancer. After treatment, she lost her hair and wore wigs. When I visited her in the nursing home she went to live in, she sat on the side of her hospital bed laughing and talking- telling stories - continuing to make everyone smile and laugh.

Looking back, she was brave and as I watched her grow weaker and weaker, I remember thinking how sad life is at moments.

As children, life was simple. We went to school, did homework, played after school, made friends, watched TV, and dreamed of being older. Older people had money and could go wherever they wanted, stay up late, and do all the things we dreamed of doing. We thought everything would be great when we were finally 'older.' The Beach Boys even sang a song, "Wouldn't it be nice if we were older..."

Since becoming older, I wish I could sit and have a chat with the adults from my childhood. I would tell them they how distressed I am because they made life look so simple and uncomplicated. They never seemed strained or worried. Time just seemed to go by easily as they did the things adults do. Now I see it all differently.

Sometimes life is filled with love and laughter and hard work pays off and all is well with the world. Other times life is challenging with sorrow and loss and grief and struggle. The longer I live, the more I have said good - bye to beloved family members and friends and pets. I have watched treasured friends falter into memory losses and struggle with health issues. Some close to me have struggled with addiction or sorrow and personal loss. As we are older, there are mortgages, car payments, bills, good and bad relationships, responsibilities- all can be challenging events in a day to day life.

Good friends and family are priceless to me because they help me muddle through the ups and downs of life. As I share with them, they share with me. It is comforting to know 'I am not alone.' We share many of the same struggles, the same ups and downs, and the same happy and sad times as many of those around us. We're in this together.

Write your story here

Buffy

We were having trouble racing. Our young horses were in training and hadn't started racing and some of our girls were hurt and couldn't race. We were newbies and others made us feel as if we did not have the talent to train a horse to race. This spurred us on to prove them wrong. We could do it! We knew we could train a horse to pace around a track with a driver in a little race bike behind them.

Some friends had many horses and offered to let us finish training one of theirs. We took Mystical Buffy on lease. If I ever had a decision to do over again, I would have purchased her. The original promise was that if we wanted her, we could have her for $1500.00. We thought this was fair.

She was a feisty girl and floated when she paced. Her daddy was a well known horse named Albert Albert. This impressed the other horsemen because folks in the racing world know every mare and stallion that ever lived. When Buffy was ready to race, her first race was at a fair. She did not win, however, she paced fast enough to qualify to race at the racetrack. Horses wanting to race were required to complete a qualifying race or a race at a fair in a minimum race time so slow horses or horses that were not prepared to race did not risk injury to themselves or others.

The first night Buffy raced at the racetrack, she won. We were elated. We had proved we could train a horse to race and win! Winning gave you the privilege of strutting around like you just won the Kentucky Derby when it was just a small race most never knew was won. It was gratifying though. An added bonus was that the racetrack videotaped all the races and offered them to owners. We purchased Buffy's WIN video.

Victory was sweet, but short lived. We lost the next ten races - we didn't even finish in the money for any of these races- the first 5 finishers receive money. We were back to discouraged.

One night I noticed my training partner watching Buffy's only WIN video in our living room. He kept playing it over and over. Others had many win videos, we just had one. A little sorrow swept over me. I wanted to tell him we would win again and have more videos. I wanted to tell him it would be 'ok.' I didn't say a word and he just kept watching the race over and over.

After a long losing streak, I pleaded with a talented driver to drive Buffy. I told him a little fib - that I knew another talented driver that recommended him. He was skeptical, but agreed to drive for us. She won! I was so excited that, when I took the horse from him and went to jump on the race bike to drive her to the win barn, I fell on the track. He giggled. I asked him if he would drive for us again and promised to fall off the race bike again if that would help him decide. He did and she went on to win many races for us.

When we made the offer to buy Buffy for the original price - after doing the training and the care- the owners more for her. We were disappointed and returned her to her original owners.

Write your story here_____

The Day Things Went Wrong

Having a thirty acre farm can be quite challenging at times. With horses, dogs, cats, chickens, ducks, and a goat, organization is a must.

One chore I actually enjoy is grass/field cutting. However, being 'just a girl,' tractor maintenance has never been on the list of one of my many talents. Once I neglected to put gear oil in the gear box of my brush hog mower and, needless to say, it locked up and has never mowed again. Another time, a friend came to check on me. He noticed I had not added water or antifreeze to the radiator. Very bad. I managed to add these prior to ruining the engine of my tractor.

I did, however, learn to change the oil in the tractor. Anyone who knows me knows this is quite an accomplishment. I was proud of myself for this even if no one felt compelled to reinforce my outstanding talents in tractor maintenance - I guess something everyone else took for granted.

One day, after changing the oil, I began mowing grass. All of the sudden, the tractor just stopped. I knew I had gas because I had just filled the tank. As I looked around the tractor parts, the vibration of the tractor over the grass made the bolt holding the oil in its compartment fall out. All the oil drained from my tractor engine. I saw oil dripping on the tractor and in a line along the grass I had just mowed. I searched the grass everywhere the tractor had just passed over and never found that bolt.

My neighbors always knew how to help me when I was in a jam. They are veteran farmers and told me to contact a tractor supply company about 20 minutes from my farm. I did, they had the bolt, and I started to the store - me and my 'everything always goes wrong for me' bad attitude.

While waiting for the salesman to finish with his other customers, another farmer came into the store. He struck up conversation and asked what happened. When I shared my story, he apparently picked up on my grumpy attitude. In a wonderfully casual and direct way, he said, 'You know, anytime you do anything, something is bound to go wrong- unless you just sit at home in a chair. But even then, you could fall off the chair.'

Immediately I was reformed. My bad attitude melted away as I realized I was not the only one challenging events happened to and just like everyone else, I could deal with things that did not go perfectly. I could fix things and get on with my chores. I thanked him for taking time to help me see my unfortunate events a little differently. I often think of that day, especially when things don't go as easily as I had planned, and I remember the only way nothing is going to go wrong is if I sit at home in a chair- and I laugh as I think I could even fall off the chair.

The salesman sold me the bolt, I purchased oil, arrived back home, replaced the bolt, put the oil in the tractor- luckily it started - and mowed the rest of my fields. Good day after all.

Write your story here____

Solomon

On January 2, 1965, the best horse in the world was born - a bay thoroughbred. He, however, did not come to be my best friend until one February afternoon in 1980. That was when I arrived at a farm in Olmsted Township, Ohio to meet him. The present owner was a young girl who found him too challenging. Her mother invited me to ride him in the indoor arena at their stable. During my ride, he was ornery and bucked like a rodeo horse all along the long wall of the arena. The mother was mortified. She looked certain I would never buy this horse. When I finished my ride, I patted his neck, rode up to her, and said, "I like him, can I make an offer?" I did. We did. And he was mine.

I named him Solomon. We rode everywhere - we jumped, did dressage, ran in the woods like he was a race horse, and had the time of our lives. I realized the first day I rode him it was dinner time. He did not want to ride, he wanted to eat. I never rode him before a meal again and he never misbehaved again.

Solomon needed extra grain because of poor care before I owned him. He and I went from barn to barn because no one would feed him properly. I was always truthful and told the new barn owner what he needed and I was willing to pay extra. I admitted I was disappointed at other barns. They took the money, but never fed him the extra feed. I was angry because I loved him and did not want him underweight.

After many attempts at a positive experience boarding Solomon, I arrived at a new barn to talk to the owner about bringing him there. The owner and I talked for a while as I looked over the stable. Then, in a snotty tone, I asked, "Are you going to feed the horse?"

I'm pretty sure she wanted to bite my head off and send me off the property without making a deal. She pursed her lips tightly and said in a firm and purposeful manner, "I'll feed the horse." She did. She was wonderful and all my past bad experiences were unfair to pass along to her and assume the worst would happen again. We became the best friends because she loved him too. She held up her end of the bargain.

As we became friends, I learned she had cancer when she was younger. She had a relapse and was battling the disease again. After sharing several years of friendship with this family, she passed. Understandably, this was very sad for all who knew her. Sol and I lost a great friend that day.

When I attended the funeral, I expressed my sympathy to her husband. He surprised me when he candidly shared his thoughts with me. He said, "You have to watch what you pray for, we prayed for 20 years, we got 23. We should have prayed for 40." I have never forgotten his words. Yes, I agree, we should ask big when asking. I have. I do. The whole family probably thought 20 years would be a great gift - and it was- it is just never enough - as I know all too well.

Write your story here___

Almost Heaven

When we were children, we visited our father's family in West Virginia each year. My two brothers and I looked forward to the vacation and have many memories of the fun we had riding in a red wagon as it rolled down little hills that looked gigantic to us as youngsters, we playing on a homemade swing in the huge tree in the front yard, turning over rocks to find copperhead and rattle snakes, and hiking the mountains behind our grandparents' home. In the evenings we joined Grandma and aunts and uncles on a yard swing and talked for hours. All great fun for young children.

Grandma cooked on a coal stove. I have one particular memory of sitting at the dinner table with relatives and my family as Grandma served scrumptious chicken and dumplings. I wanted more and more. She also made banana pudding with vanilla cookies.

When I was grown, my family relocated to West Virginia- to a farm very close to my grandparents' farm. The scenery seemed different. The hills in grandma's yard looked smaller and smaller each year and the swing ropes looked shorter and shorter. My parents became farmers. They had a large garden and horses, pigs, and chickens. Often my mother had injured animals in the house. One visit she had a chicken with an injured leg in the house. Mostly she kept the hen in a cage, but let her roam the house occasionally.

One day, my brother and I were sitting on the couch in the living room talking. We hardly noticed the chicken strutting casually around the house. He proudly shook the rattle of a dead rattlesnake he found a few days earlier. We were listening to the 'rattle' when, suddenly, the chicken (who was supposed to be injured) jumped up, grabbed the rattle from my brother's hand, and ran away with it. Running as fast as she could, she darted back and forth into the kitchen- her little eyes wide with excitement.

Immediately, my brother jumped off the couch and ran after that chicken. I laughed as I watched him chasing her until he caught her and recovered his rattle. After he had time to settle down, we laughed and have been telling the story for years.

I have many precious memories of visits to family in West Virginia- we called it Almost Heaven.

Write your story here_____

Jumping to Conclusions

    I was assigned to castrate 3 appaloosa horses for a client. When I arrived at the farm, the couple who owned the horses were quite pleasant and we talked for a short while before beginning the surgeries.

    When I do this surgery, I prefer to put the horse on the ground and pull one rear leg forward by tying it to a rope around the horse's neck then I complete the castration. Surgery went perfectly for the first horse, however, midway through surgery on the second horse, things did not go so well. He stood up with his leg tied. There's a first time for every disaster I always say. I administered

additional medication to put him back on the ground. He fell on the opposite side, so I pulled the other back leg forward and tied it to the rope around his neck. I finished the castration.
Yes! Both back legs were tied in a forward position at this time. I finished, untied both legs, let him wake up, and prepared to castrate the last horse.

Before we started the third horse, the owners asked to take a break and went into their home. As I waited for them to return, crazy thoughts went through my mind. I thought they were calling my boss to tell him they did not want me to do the last castration because I had so much trouble keeping the second horse down. I thought they were planning to tell me to leave their farm. The fearful thoughts were overwhelming.

When they came out, he said, "My wife and I were talking about you."

I prepared for the worst as I thought, 'I knew it! Here it comes.'

Then he said, "We really like you, you don't talk down to us. You talk like a regular person." I was so relieved and said, "I thought you were upset with me and calling the boss because I had to give a second dose of medication to the second horse."

They replied, "Oh, no. We weren't upset about that, he (the boss) had to give additional medication to a horse down THREE times one day to complete a castration."

I was amazed. It makes me think I am the only one difficult moments happen to when others don't admit circumstances don't always go perfectly for them. As time goes on I realize everyone has difficulties and no one has perfect moments every moment.

Write your story here___

Super Heroes

Many of us have a favorite Superhero. We admire their super powers - Superman with his ability to fly, super strength, and the ability to leap from tall buildings, Spiderman with his ability to scale tall buildings, swing from building to building, tie the bad guys up with his webs, or Batman in his bat-mobile fighting crime in Gotham city. What they have in common is they use their super powers for good.

In real life, I see superheroes all around. I met some of them in the halls of long term care facilities and patient rooms. I witnessed their superpowers of love and kindness as I spotted them fixing the ladies hair, picking out favorite outfits, making sure the men were shaved, and doing every other little task to make these residents' lives nice. I saw them singing to patients, playing games, reading to some, sitting beside windows and talking for hours, and feeding others.

Other superheroes I have come to know are moms and dads of special needs children struggling with various physical conditions- from muscular dystrophy to paralysis to cerebral palsy and more. Parents and grandparents who care for these children day after day have always made me appreciate how love drives those in life to do what others may consider difficult or impossible. These heroes care for their little ones - taking them to frequent doctor or hospital visits, going through all the ups and downs of medical issues that arise, and kiss them and love them all day long.

Some superheroes care for aging parents or mates or injured family members day after day. One superhero came to my life as a friend. His wife later told me how he felt I was alone and he wanted them to 'take me under their wings.' They frequently invited me to dinner and walks in the park, made wooden jumping poles for my horses, shared every achievement with me, bought equipment they knew me and my horses would cherish, drove me and my injured horse to the veterinary clinic in Columbus, Ohio, and were there for me in many, many ways. Over the years I realized I never recognized the love I was shown specially by my friends. They were superheroes sent to make my life better.

Many make sacrifices and consider their care routine and just part of each day. I have come to realize that sometimes we do not change situations. Disability is still present, worsening medical conditions, addictions, struggles, etc, may remain but we have the ability to use our superpowers of love and kindness and patience and hard work to ease the suffering and struggle of others.

One favorite story I remember goes like this - a man was walking down the road and happened upon a robin lying on its back, with its feet in the air. "Cock Robin, why are you lying on your back in the middle of the road?" the man asked. "The sky is falling, the sky is falling!" Cock Robin replied. "But why are your feet sticking up in the air?" the man pressed. "Because," said the little bird, "one must do what one can."

Write your story here

Broken Pieces/ Broken People

One of my favorite things to do in Florida is walk the beaches searching for shells. I never realized shells have specific names- like tarantella, yellow land snail, florida welk, scallops, telescopium, angel wings or concus aulicus- to name a few. I simply call them clam shells, conchs, spiral shells, and pretty ones. Once I found a sand dollar and a starfish. Friends enjoy showing me the shells they found.

Of all the shells I find, the ones I treasure most are the broken ones. I find more fragments of shells than perfect, whole shells. I collect the fragments of shells to add to shell crafts because I think they are still beautiful.

The broken shells remind me of me- broken and imperfect. So many times I catch myself saying exactly what I did not want to say. I wish I had the opportunity to relive moments and do them better a second time around. Why did I become impatient? Why did I give someone the impression I had no time for them? Why did I need to feel superior to someone else? Regretting moments is an ongoing battle. New Year's Eve is approaching. I want to be better. I want those around me know how much I appreciate them, how kind and helpful they are to me and how they make my life better just being in it. I want to choose words that let them know they are valuable and worthwhile.

Sometimes the broken shells remind me of people I love. It seems easier to accept imperfection in myself than those around me. I want them to know I see the beauty in them, the value in them. This New Year's I want to be patient and kind. I want to believe the best in all around me and never notice if anyone does wrong to me. I want them to know they are special to me- every moment, every day. I want to be there to share their struggles as well as their celebrations.

A thanks- to those who have seen me at my best and at my worst and cannot tell the difference because they love me so much. I want to love everyone else the same.

Write your story here_____

Black Duck

A friend brought me a pair of black ducks. I was told they were Muscovy ducks, but I am not certain if that was true, however, they were lovely. When the sun shone on their black feathers, the blue, green and purple colors glistened through.

The male and female were an inseparable couple. One sad day, I lost the female. I learned ducks don't like to be alone. When his mate left, he tagged along with other ducks on the farm until, one by one, I lost them as well.

I saw him lying next to the dogs and even the cats just to be near someone, something. His loneliness broke my heart since he was desperate for a friend, I decided he needed a duck pal. A friend, who had many ducks, gave me a white duck. When I arrived back at the farm, I took the new duck out of the cage he rode in in the back of my truck and introduced him to my black duck – which was waiting by the truck. They were instant friends.

Black and White did everything together- including getting into trouble together. When I couldn't find them, I immediately knew they walked down our 500 foot driveway, crossed the busy street we lived on, and waddled through the neighbor's yard to take a dip in their pond.

Thankfully, the neighbors never seemed to mind my coming to their yard, going behind their home, calling my boys out of their pond, and herding them out of their yard, across the street, and down our 500 foot driveway back to their barn.

We lived in coyote country, so each night I called the boys. They quacked and waddled themselves into the barn into a stall opened for them. I closed them in for safety each night and they knew the routine.

Sadly, the white duck passed. It was so heartbreaking I left his body in the corner of the stall he was in when he passed. For days the black duck went into the stall, sat next to him, and looked at him. He seemed confused as to why his friend no longer came with him to eat bugs and walk around our farm. He seemed to say, "Are we going to play? Why aren't you coming?" Eventually I removed the white duck and found a chicken for Black to be friends with.

I have sweet memories of friendship and love between some silly ducks and chickens I had the pleasure of having as pets.

Write your story here

Orphaned

I was called to an Amish farm to treat a large draft horse mare with colic- abdominal pain. She was in the lower area of the bank barn and had a foal with her. My exam included inspecting the horse from head to hoof and then listening to the horse's abdomen and rectally palpating to determine if there was an impaction, twisted intestines, or gas filled intestines. After examining her, I decided to pass a tube into her nose that extended to her stomach so I could give her mineral oil. When I realized I forgot to put the pump I used to pump oil and water through the tube, I told the farmer I needed to go to my farm to retrieve the pump.

I was only away a short time since my farm was close, but when I arrived back at the Amish farm, the mare was not alive. I was stunned. She never gave me any indication she was that ill. Since she was too large for men to remove, the Amish man had the mare hooked up to team of draft horses to take her out of the cramped lower barn area. He never seemed upset. Amish are accustomed to loss.

As we discussed the foal, suddenly, without being asked, the team began dragging the mare's body around the corner and out the back door of the barn. The Amish man ran after them, calling for them to stop. It was a sad scene on one hand, but, on the other hand, a little funny - one sad funny site.

He successfully stopped the team and we continued discussing the foal. I offered my foal milk replacer to help the orphan foal. I was certain she would drink from a bowl. When I returned with the replacer, the Amish man had introduced the orphan foal with another mare nursing a foal of her own. The mare graciously accepted the orphan, allowing her to nurse. Her own foal, however, was not as accepting.

The orphan foal nursed on the mare's one side and the mare's baby on the other. I watched the mare's baby move around the back of the mare and, when he spotted the orphan, he pinned his ears, bucked a little, and moved back to his side of the mare. It seemed if the orphan was 'out of sight, out of mind' all was ok. The orphan seemed oblivious and continued to nurse. It must be difficult to share your mother, but it must also be difficult to lose your mother. The mare raised both foals and all ended well.

Write your story here____

Pretty Clothes

As a younger girl, I pursued education - which meant I had a meager budget. I usually attended classes in T-shirts and blue jeans but, like most girls, I loved pretty clothes.

I rode the bus from my grandfather's home to the Square in downtown Cleveland every day for school. When I arrived at the Square, there were department stores like ones in the movies – ones with many floors and counters lined with jewelry and perfumes and gloves and matching scarves that were soft and beautiful. I am convinced I was the best window shopper ever.

I walked around the cases admiring all the new accessories. Then, I rode the escalator to shopper's heaven- to the floors with rack after rack of shorts and matching tops, skirts, and blouses, and all the pretty clothes one could imagine.

I picked several outfits and spent time in the dressing room trying on these beautiful clothes I knew I would never buy. I modeled them in the mirror and, for a moment, I was wearing something pretty. After a time daydreaming and admiring, I donned my T-shirt and blue jeans and returned the clothes to the rack. The salesladies smiled and nicely asked if I wanted to buy anything. I smiled back and said, "I am going to think about it some more, thanks." I suspected they knew.

Then I walked 20 blocks, attended class, walked back to the bus, and rode back to my grandfather's home- remembering my wonderful time window shopping- which I did frequently.

I still love pretty things, but have realized I want the inside of me to be more lovely than the outside and really have no extra money for extravagant things. That's ok. I have a wonderful country to enjoy that allows me beautiful adventures every day and family and friends that mean everything to me. I have made the choice to make the people in my life my priority and have no regrets. I still see the pretty clothes and think of my days shopping, but more and more the clothes mean less and less and the people mean more and more.

Write your story here_____

Singe

I recently accepted employment at a private practice where I met Singe. At first I thought he was some fancy purebred cat - with small ears and different coloring around his eyes. I couldn't have been more wrong. Singe is a mutt- a plain old alley cat. But he had a story.

Singe was a man of the streets. He had to hunt his own food, find shelter in the very hot, humid temperatures of Florida as well as the torrential rains that occur daily in the summer time. He had to hide from others who would hurt him and no one was there to help with his medical needs or care about him in any way. All that was about to change.

During a localized fire in the brush of Florida, the responding firemen found a black and white cat under a bush. His little ears were burned and his facial hair singed. The pads of his paws were injured from the fire and he was frightened. The only home he knew in the forest was on fire and he didn't know what to do.

The firemen knew what to do. They scooped him up and took him to the veterinary clinic he now calls his home. He was nursed to health by the veterinarians and technicians who work there. They treated his burns and cared for him until he healed. Now, he no longer has to go farther the next room for a meal, everyone there loves him and meets all his physical and medical needs, massages him with special made tools to do so, and allows him to think he owns the place.

Singe bears all the scars that serve as reminders that there are wonderful and caring people in the world who take time to rescue little animals from danger so they can have a story to tell everyone. Singe is a testament to the spirit of survival and healing and the will and desire to live - even after it looked like everything was lost. His tragedy turned to triumph for this little overweight pampered cat called Singe.

Write your story here_____

Language

I've only known how to speak one language.

My brother was asked to give a speech on words once. He shared how he considered this assignment difficult and couldn't think of what to say. I decided I would have said that words mean everything. Words convey love, encouragement, sympathy, hope, well wishing, congratulations, and trust - not only to humans, but animals as well. We've all been taught to 'choose our words wisely.'

When training horses, we use 'aides.' Aides include hands on the reins to communicate to the horse, legs on their sides- also to communicate, shifting weight sends messages, and sometimes an artificial aide-such as a crop or spurs is used.

Another aide I rely on is my voice. Tone conveys good, bad, emergent, reassuring, and calming messages to horses as well as most animals. Horses are able to learn words such as trot, canter, walk, and 'ho' for stop. This is apparent when instructors ask riders to command the horse, and, at the words of the instructor, the horse obeys the words before the rider executes the request. Some instructors change the words for basic commands to avoid this, but smart horses learn the new words as well.

Emily was blind in one eye. Once, while jogging, she kicked at a fly and broke one driving line. This became an emergency because she followed the unbroken line in a large circle and, if she continued, this would have resulted in her crashing into the barn. I asked her to 'ho.' She stopped in the middle of the field she had drifted into and stood as I safely got off the jog cart and led her back to the barn without disaster.

Another day, Mattie and I were jogging when she kicked up at a fly and one leg went over the shaft of the jog cart - she straddled the shaft. I asked her to stop on the track. She did allowing me to remove her harness, free her from the cart, move her leg over the lowered shaft, put her harness back on, reattach the cart to the harness, and allowed me to get back onto the jog cart to continue jogging. She calmly obeyed even though other horses jogged by her. This is amazing trust because racing horses are often excited to race when around other horses. Mattie stood with me quietly and calmly as I asked her to.

Write your story here_____

Reputation

I have enjoyed a pretty respectable and valuable reputation. Most consider me the 'good girl.'

However, one night while employed with the ambulance, we just finished transferring a patient to an emergency room with a parking lane recessed to the door.

After delivering the patient, I decided to move the ambulance. Since there was a car blocking the path in front of me, I decided to back up the ramp behind me. I turned to check my mirrors and noticed they were not adjusted properly. I ignored the fact I could not see what was behind me, put the ambulance in reverse, and gunned the gas pedal. CRASH!!

Oops! As I got out to look, there, sitting in the passenger seat of the police car I hit, was an officer. I sized up the damage to my bumper and rear panel and his broken windshield.

He gave me a look as if to say, "really?"

I leaned in the driver's window and asked, 'What are my chances of us pretending this never happened?' with my 'Please feel sorry for me and forgive me' look.

He thought about it for a moment, shrugged his shoulders, and said, 'Pretty good.'

We both knew the city would repair the vehicles and we didn't want to fill out any paperwork.

I didn't want to be blamed for the damage, so I backed the ambulance into our regular parking spot so the damage was hidden from immediate view. When the oncoming crew arrived, they usually inspected the ambulance. Apparently, they didn't notice the damage.

During the new crew's shift, they responded to an emergency. When they brought their patient to the back of the ambulance to load them for transport, they noticed the damage. They thought someone hit them while they were inside. I giggled thinking they might have heard a crash like that. It never occurred to them to think I had anything to do with the damage. I never said a word. The ambulance was repaired and I certain the police car was also.

My good reputation paid off.

Write your story here

In Search of Christmas

    I love Christmas. I decorate trees, find a special new ornament each year, set out my nativities- a collection I am proud of, and send Christmas cards to family and friends. I decorate the outside of the house and bushes and scan magazines and library books for Christmas crafts. I spend hours in front of the television watching holiday movies and look forward to family time as well as time with friends. I enjoy finding the perfect gifts for everyone. My radio station plays non-stop Christmas music - a treat I look forward to each year. In short, I love it all. I am one of those who wishes it could be Christmas 365 days a year!

    My friends and family do a cookie swap each year. I am always assigned the oatmeal cookies because everyone is aware of my baking limitations. I enjoy the great meals with pumpkin and apple pies. We attend church on Christmas Eve and include others to share our holiday that may not have family to spend time with.

But when I think about Christmas, I realize the reason I love Christmas so much is because of the real meaning of the season. It is the time I get to thank God for sending His very best. My search for Christmas does not take me to a palace with plush royalty and all the comforts of wealth. My search takes me to a much different and unusual place. In find Christmas in a manger- where my Savior was a Baby born to a peasant girl who believed the angel of God who told her she would be the mother of Jesus and not to be afraid. There was no room in the inn, so I find Him in that stable one quiet, holy night thousands of years ago. He was wrapped in swaddling clothes and visited by a few shepherds. Wise men traveled far to see Him.

I have found Christmas. I have made the choice to be one of the wise people that still seek Jesus. I know the reason for the season. He is my King and the Baby born to live and die for all to live. Glory to God in the Highest and on Earth, peace and good will toward men.

Write what Christmas means to you.

Write your story here____

Day for Surgery

Draft horses are beautiful, but it is no understatement- they are BIG.

I was asked to a farmer's home to anesthetize a yearly draft horse so an Amish man could perform a castration surgery. This was a little irregular, but I understood. Amish are skilled at certain tasks, however, they have no way of obtaining medications for anesthesia. This owner wanted my help for this.

This was the first time I was asked to drop a horse in a stall - what we refer to as giving anesthesia and laying the horse on the ground. I usually chose to do the surgery on large grassy areas or in large open indoor arenas with soft, dry footing - my reasons for doing so are these areas are easier to work in as well as if the horse falls on the 'right' side, they can be flipped to the 'left' side by grabbing the hooves and all at once, flipping him. The 'side' the horse falls on is important because if the surgeon is right handed, the instruments come into the scrotal area from behind and any possible injury to the genitals is avoided.

    I estimated the weight of the yearly colt to be approximately 2,200 pounds and administered my sedation medication followed by short acting anesthetic medication. He then proceeded to drop on his right side and could not be flipped in the small stall. The Amish man was as uncomfortable about the horse being on his right side as I am, so he and the owner asked me to complete the castration.

    Immediately I ran to my truck and quickly opened the compartments, grabbed the bucket and the emasculator (the tool used to castrate the horse), some soap and sponges, a blade, gloves, and some water and ran back to the horse. I prepped the skin of the scrotum and began surgery. I made my first incision over the right testicle but when I tried to remove it, the muscle that raises and lowers the testicle in the scrotum was pulling harder than I was able to pull. I pulled with all my strength and couldn't remove that testicle. Since this wasn't working, I had the not so bright idea to try removing the other testicle. I couldn't remove that one either. I could only imagine what the two men watching were thinking.

    I quit trying, leaned up against the stall wall, and told the owner I needed to let him stand and give him a second dose of anesthesia. Luckily, he fell on his left side this time and as I began to castrate him, I saw the wood shavings used as bedding in his stall covering the incisions I made. I hesitated for a moment and thought 'fabulous,' tried to clean as much as I could, and continued the surgery, ignoring this complication that could lead to infection.

After struggling to remove those testicles, I finally finished the surgery. I stood, exhausted and shaking. The owner was sweet and smiled as he patted me on the shoulder, and said, "You did it!" I was certainly glad it was over and I am sure he was too.

The colt's surgery was on Thursday. When I arrived back at work the following Monday, during our morning reports to the boss, my fellow vet said he ran into a horse owner on Saturday who said he just came from a horse funeral - a recently castrated Belgian yearly. I sat speechless and sure I had misunderstood. My face was as white as a sheet and I think my heart almost stopped. My fellow vet was unable to keep a straight face and then said, 'He said to tell her (me) he was just kidding - and tell Teri she did a great job.' I was relieved to know the horse was okay. The men thought they were very funny. I probably would have thought it was all pretty funny too if it happened to someone else. Funny how that is sometimes.

Write your story here_____

Tammy From Miami

Tammy's Sable was a birthday gift. She was a Standard bred horse born for racing. Most would consider this an odd sort of gift, but to me, it was the best gift ever. She only cost $550.00 because she was tiny - not as tiny as the little one above- but tiny. Everyone ridiculed me for wanting her, but I didn't care.

I loved her like she was a big and talented racing horse. The funny thing was, she moved like the wind and she had a heart as big as any big horse. Her small size made my partner comfortable. I was new to training harness racing horses, and, as a matter of fact, I really didn't know how. One day while at a continuing education meeting for my veterinary license, the speaker was a whale trainer from Sea World. Most seminars are boring, but will never forget this one.

The trainer - who trained whales to jump out of the water with him standing or sitting on their noses - mentioned training racing horses and what to do while training them. I decided that if he knew how to make whales do what he made them do, I would do what he advised about training racing horses. I did and it worked. Tammy was my guinea pig- so to speak.

She raced so well other horsemen wanted to buy her from me. They would tell me how they watched her jut her head forward, flap her lower lip, and pace away. I enjoyed watching my horse, but it was nice to know others did as well. She was so small our driver told us he had difficulty keeping her from sneaking under the arms of the start car before the start car passed over the start line to let all the horses go. She won at the racetrack and at county fairs and raced for 5 years.

The announcer made comments like, 'Here comes Tammy Sable with her little legs just a churning,' and 'Watch out, they're racing Shetland ponies out there tonight,' and 'Here comes Tammy Sable to the winner's circle- making her driver look ten feet tall' because he was a shorter man. I never met that announcer, but I wanted to tell him that was MY horse he was talking about that way. I know he was just having fun and so was Tammy.

One race I told her driver to not let her get locked in- she needed to be out on the outside of the pack of horses or she would be trying so hard to race she would hurt herself. No one believed me until they drove her. She won a race in Delaware, Ohio leaving the gate first and came across the finish line first- I was so excited, you would have thought we won the Little Brown Jug- the race like the Kentucky Derby for harness horses.

    One particular night another horseman bragged all day his horse could not be beat that night. We were in his race. A groom walked by me and Tammy in the race stall and I heard him loudly say, "DID YOU SEE HOW LITTLE THE FOUR HORSE IS?" We were the 4 horse. I covered Tammy's ears and told her she was going to have to ignore all those guys and beat them all tonight just to show them all she was not just the littlest horse in the field tonight- she was the best. When she raced, she was so small we couldn't see her behind the other horses, but when she made her way around the last turn, we saw her little nose out in front and those little legs were a churning and her lower lip was flapping and she pulled away from all the boys and all the big horses as she led the pack down the last stretch and she was first over the finish line that night. Everyone saw how little the 4 horse was that night.

    She was my Tammy from Miami- this was my little pet name for her when we exercised. I think of all the fun we had and how she was just my little tiny birthday gift.

Write your story here_____

Tell everyone your story!